THE OFFICE OF
PRIME MINISTER

THE OFFICE OF
PRIME MINISTER

BY

LORD BLAKE

Provost of The Queen's College, Oxford
Fellow of the Academy

THANK-OFFERING TO
BRITAIN FUND LECTURES
1974

PUBLISHED FOR THE BRITISH ACADEMY
BY OXFORD UNIVERSITY PRESS
1975

Oxford University Press, Ely House, London W. 1

GLASGOW   NEW YORK   TORONTO   MELBOURNE   WELLINGTON
CAPE TOWN   IBADAN   NAIROBI   DAR ES SALAAM   LUSAKA   ADDIS ABABA
DELHI   BOMBAY   CALCUTTA   MADRAS   KARACHI   LAHORE   DACCA
KUALA LUMPUR   SINGAPORE   HONG KONG   TOKYO

ISBN 0 19 725724 0

*Printed in Great Britain
at the University Press, Oxford
by Vivian Ridler
Printer to the University*

CONTENTS

I. THE PERSONALITIES

To be 'Prime Minister of England', if one can use the old-fashioned phrase without offending against the Race Relations Act, has always been the goal of aspiring politicians since the office first came into being. The unique status of the post is well conveyed by Macaulay writing to his father when Canning died in August 1827 after only four months in office.

> To fall at the very moment of reaching the very highest pinnacle of human ambition! The whole work of thirty chequered years of glory and obloquy struck down in a moment! The noblest prize that industry, dexterity, wit and eloquence ever obtained vanishing into nothing in the very instant in which it had been grasped.[1]

And with a sort of fearful inevitability Macaulay ends 'Vanity of vanities—all is vanity'.

In their hearts probably most Prime Ministers have thought of their office in a solemn light, even if they have not quite said so. Sir Winston Churchill later wrote of his own elevation in May 1940, 'I felt as if I were walking with destiny and that all my past life had been but a preparation for this hour and for this trial'.[2] Stanley Baldwin asked those who congratulated him to give him their prayers. Gladstone was busy cutting down a tree at Hawarden Castle when a telegram was brought out to him announcing the imminent arrival of the Queen's Private Secretary. 'Very significant', he observed and attacked the tree again.

---

[1] Thomas Pinney (ed.), *Letters of T. B. Macaulay*, i (1974), p. 224.
[2] Winston S. Churchill, *The Gathering Storm* (1948), pp. 526–7.

After a few minutes he paused and in tones of 'deep earnestness' addressed his companion, 'My mission', he exclaimed, 'is to pacify Ireland'.[1] One is inclined to echo Macaulay 'Vanity of vanities . . .!' Disraeli, as one would expect, was flippant and slightly cynical. He had, he told a friend 'climbed to the top of the greasy pole at last'. But who can doubt that he felt with intensity the romance and glamour of his strange situation and that he viewed with secret relish the survey of his own extraordinary career?

As for Melbourne, outwardly even more world-weary and cynical than Disraeli, he was, we are told, inclined to regard the office as 'a damned bore' and was in two minds whether to accept, till his secretary, 'Ubiquity' Young, persuaded him with the immortal words: 'Why damn it such a position was never occupied by any Greek or Roman, and, if it only lasts two months it is well worth while to have been Prime Minister of England.'[2] But one may venture to doubt whether Melbourne's first reaction was really quite as casual as it seems. He too, I suspect, like Disraeli, was not impervious to the excitement and drama of the chance that was offered to him. He would probably have taken it, without being reminded of Greece and Rome. After all even Mr. Attlee observes in his memoirs that 26 July 1945, the occasion of Labour's victory and his summons to the Palace, was an 'exciting day', although it has to be admitted that his own account of it does not sound very exciting.

The office of Prime Minister has been one of the most important constitutional developments which have spread from Britain to a very large part of that section of the world governed by free institutions. To speak about it in this series of lectures—'Thank-offering to Britain'—is therefore

[1] John Morley, *Life of Gladstone* (1903), p. 252.
[2] Lytton Strachey and Roger Fulford (eds.), *The Greville Memoirs*, iii (1938), p. 76.

appropriate. But it would be wrong to suppose that the British Cabinet system of which the Prime Ministership is such an essential feature is the only way in which a liberal democracy can operate. The American model, the most important alternative, although based largely on what was then believed to be a purified version of the British system, is very different and not less effective. The American colonies broke away just before the characteristic features of the Cabinet system in Britain had emerged in a clear and obvious form. They were certainly in existence but only behind a façade which concealed them, and some of what became the most successful aspects of British government were connected by the dissident Americans with the worst defects of monarchical rule under George III.

There are therefore two quite distinct types of liberal government in the world. On the whole in Europe, where liberal government exists at all, it is on the British model, e.g. most of the E.E.C. countries and Scandinavia; the title of Prime Minister is used even in countries which are anything but liberal such as those east of the Iron Curtain. In India, in the 'white' ex-Colonies—Canada, South Africa, Rhodesia, Australasia—the Cabinet system also prevails even though its practical working may be sometimes very different from its prototype. In these countries a distinction still exists between the Head of State as a ceremonial and symbolic figure analogous to the British monarch, and the head of a Cabinet which is the real wielder of power and authority. In South America the American presidential model has on the whole prevailed, also in a large part of Black Africa where the separation between nominal and real authority has never seemed to make sense. In many of these countries the Presidential system is as much a cloak for authoritarian rule, as the Prime Ministerial system is in eastern Europe.

The country most difficult to categorize is France. It is

a mixture of Cabinet and Presidential government established, as new constitutions usually are, to suit a particular situation, the crisis of 1958, and a particular individual, General de Gaulle. We should not be surprised at this. What else was our own settlement after the Glorious Revolution of 1688? But it will be fascinating to see how it will develop, how deep its roots will strike, and whether, like so many French constitutions since 1789, it will wither away and be replaced by a new one, or whether it will provide a lasting framework for the evolution of French politics.

But I am not attempting in these lectures to deal with these wider aspects of the development of the office of Prime Minister. I wish to confine myself to Britain, the country of its origin, and to examine the sort of people who have been Prime Ministers, the way the office has developed historically, and finally the situation as it is today with perhaps some glance at future prospects.

I thought I would begin with a survey of the men—there has not yet been a woman—who have held the office. In my first lecture, therefore, I am hoping to give some sort of 'profile'. What was their class, economic and educational background? How old were they when they were appointed? How long was their tenure? Do these facts simply reflect in a given period the social structure of Britain in that period or is there something more to it than that? Does the composite portrait of Prime Ministers which one might thus draw last beyond the particular era of a particular group and show features in common over the far longer period during which the office has existed? Or must one merely take half a century or so at a time and say that Prime Ministers were of such and such a character during that period, and of such and such during the next—one portrait for 1800 to 1850, and another for 1850 to 1900 let us say?

Before going into this we have to settle the important question of how long the post of Prime Minister has existed—a subject of much controversy and dispute. Mr. Ehrman in his admirable first volume of his life of the younger Pitt cites Beatson's *Political Index* of 1786 giving the list of 'Prime Ministers and Favourites from the Accession of Henry VIII to the Present Time'. Since 1714 Beatson could only find one 'Sole Minister', and that was Sir Robert Walpole.[1] At all subsequent periods he feels that he has to bracket two, three, or even four people as joint or co-equal ministers whose advice the King took and who therefore controlled the governance of the country. The difficulty is emphasized by the fact that from 1721 to 1782 there is no instance of the sort of 'clean sweep' which one expects when a modern Prime Minister is defeated and resigns. Even Walpole's departure from office did not carry all his colleagues with him. It is not till the resignation of Lord North that we have a clear break. With the exception of the Lord Chancellor the new administration under Lord Rockingham consisted entirely of new men. Thereafter it makes sense to talk of the Rockingham, the Shelburne, the Pitt, the Addington administration and to make a list of members of 'the Cabinet' which is at last beginning to emerge with a less shadowy outline from the mists of mid eighteenth-century practice. Yet there would seem something perverse and contrary to common sense in nominating Rockingham as the 'first Prime Minister' simply for this reason.

It would probably be agreed by most historians that in the search for that elusive entity one at least need not go back beyond Sir Robert Walpole. Whether or not he deserves the title, no one before him does. The difficulty about Walpole, and his successors till the end of the century and perhaps even beyond, is that the monarch

[1] *The Younger Pitt*, i (1969), p. 183.

was still in a very real sense the head of the executive. It was from him that the separate departments of state derived their authority–departments which were self-contained with long-established traditions of their own, extremely jealous of one another, and determined not to be encroached upon. Their heads were answerable to the King, not to any 'Sole' or other minister. The King appointed them and dismissed them, as of course in theory the Crown does today. But whereas today these appointments or dismissals are in reality made by the Prime Minister, in the eighteenth century this was not necessarily the case at all. Hence even a minister, with the strength and longevity in office of Walpole, occupied a very different position from, let us say, that of Sir Robert Peel. The office as held by Peel was much more like its counterpart of today than its namesake of a hundred years before.

I shall, however, stick to tradition and count Walpole as the first of his line. Whatever else is obscure, no one can dispute that Walpole's ministry marks a change from the circumstances of those preceding him. He was able to overcome the chronic past difficulty of the Crown and, for that matter even the Lord Protector–the problem of how to control an increasingly turbulent, almost anarchical, Parliament. Before Walpole ministers depended entirely upon the confidence of the monarch, and did their best often with very limited success to cope with a violently partisan and often hostile Parliament. Walpole found the means denied to his predecessors of controlling Parliament. This did not mean that he could do without the support of the Crown. Far from it. In the words of Professor Plumb, in his distinguished Ford Lectures, describing the new system thus established:

Essential though it was to possess the confidence of the King, domination of Parliament proved more important. When at

last Walpole failed to do so he went. By then, however, his
system was so strong that it made little or no difference. The
Whig aristocracy remained in power.[1]

We now come to the problem posed by Beatson in the
quotation which I gave earlier. Between 1714 and 1786
is it right to regard Walpole as the one and only 'sole
Minister'? It seems to me wrong to put him into that
unique position. After all what else was the younger Pitt
himself when Beatson was writing? Although there are
difficulties, it seems on the whole best to regard the First
Lord of the Treasury as Prime Minister, unless there is
some palpable reason to the contrary. It was, after all, the
vital post with its control over patronage and finance,
especially when doubled with that of Chancellor of the
Exchequer, as was the normal practice whenever the First
Lord sat in the House of Commons. There is, however, one
obvious exception. William Pitt the elder, later Earl of
Chatham, was never First Lord of the Treasury. In what
would be regarded as *his* ministries he was Secretary of
State for the Southern Department from December 1756
to April 1757, and again from June 1757 to October 1761,
and Lord Privy Seal from July 1766 to November 1768.
I shall count him as Prime Minister for those periods.
Happily this does not exclude the three Dukes, Devonshire,
Newcastle, and Grafton who were First Lords of the
Treasury at the time, for in each case at least a part of their
period in office was spent without the presence of Pitt. On
these assumptions one can say that in 253 years there
have been forty-nine Prime Ministers.

What kind of a picture can we construct in terms of
age, tenure, education, social position, etc., over the
course of two and a half centuries? Age has varied enormously. William Pitt at 24 is, of course, famous as the

---

[1] *The Growth of Political Stability in England 1675–1725* (1967), p. 179.

youngest to enter his high office for the first time, and few come anywhere near him—the Duke of Grafton at 33 and Lord Rockingham at 35 being the closest. The only others to achieve it under forty were the Duke of Devonshire and Lord North. At the other end of the scale Palmerston was 70, Campbell-Bannerman 69. (The latter, incidentally, has a claim to be the 'first Prime Minister' since he was the first person to be so described in an official document, but this is really only a formal point.) Neville Chamberlain and Lord Aberdeen were 68. No less than fourteen Prime Ministers have taken office for the first time at an age above that nowadays deemed to be appropriate for civil servants to retire, and seven have done so over the age at which even schoolmasters are put out to grass.

Of course if we count Prime Ministers who continued in office beyond either of those ages the number is much larger. Gladstone holds the record. Having declared in 1874 that he longed for an interval of quiet between Parliament and the grave, he finally retired from the scene nineteen years later at 84. Both Palmerston and Churchill, neither of whom made any such statement of intent, passed eighty, before death in the one case and retirement in the other brought their careers to a close.

The average age of Prime Ministers on first appointment is $52\frac{1}{2}$. But there has been a change over the years. The first twenty-four of our forty-nine, from Walpole to the end of Grey's administration in 1834, averaged slightly below 47. The twenty-five since then were markedly older, by over a decade—the average being slightly under 59. In fact the trend had begun rather earlier. Canning who took office in 1827 at the age of 57 was the oldest man to do so since the Duke of Newcastle in 1754.

Averages can be misleading. I can find only one Prime Minister who actually took office at the age of 52 to 53. That is Lord Derby. The most common quinquennium is

45 to 50. Eleven Prime Ministers were appointed between those ages. The runner-up is 55 to 60 in which
there are nine. The commonest single year of age is 46
(five).

Tenure of office has varied no less widely than age of
entry. Walpole in power for slightly under twenty-one
years still holds the record, with the younger Pitt, in
office for nearly nineteen, as the nearest rival. After them
we have Liverpool with over fourteen years, Salisbury
with just under, and Gladstone with twelve. At the other
end of the scale there is William Pulteney, Earl of Bath,
whose ill-fated attempt lasted only two days from 10–12
February 1746. Pulteney was First Lord and Carteret held
the seals of both Secretaryships of State but no one else
would join. A contemporary 'squib' entitled 'A History of
the Long Administration' concludes:

And thus endeth the second and last part of this astonishing
Administration which lasted forty-eight hours and three
quarters, seven minutes, and eleven seconds; which may truly
be called the most honest of all administrations; the minister
to the astonishment of all wise men never transacted one rash
thing; and, what is more marvellous left as much money in
the Treasury as he found in it.[1]

Scarcely longer was Earl Waldegrave's unhappy venture
in 1757, which began on 8 June and ended on 12 June.
One might argue that these should not count at all, but
in each case the individuals were actually appointed, and
so I think they ought to figure on the list which is of
Prime Ministers not just of successful ones.

By the same token, though it does not affect these
figures, we should count the brief 'second administration'
of the Duke of Wellington November–December 1834
which existed for some three weeks while Britain awaited

---

[1] *Dictionary of National Biography*, iii, p. 1122 (entry for Carteret).

the return of Sir Robert Peel from Rome where he was on holiday when William IV inconveniently and unpredictably got rid of Melbourne. The Duke duly kissed hands as First Lord of the Treasury, and held for good measure as well the seals of Secretary of State for Foreign Affairs, Home Affairs, and the Colonies. He made a point of seeing that the clerks were attending to their duties. Of course he resigned as soon as Peel was back, but if Peel had expired in a carriage accident or had fallen off the Channel Packet Wellington might very easily have had to continue as a 'real' Prime Minister. Certainly the initiative would have been in his hands.

The average tenure of office is five years and two months, but as with age of appointment, it is a statistical abstraction. Peel is the only Prime Minister who actually held office for that length of time and Lloyd George the only other to be in the five- to six-year bracket. The most frequent bracket is three to four years (nine) followed oddly enough by under one year (eight). Twenty-eight Prime Ministers held office for under four years, twelve for between four and eight years, and nine for more than eight. There seems to be no obvious change in these patterns during the period, although the average tenure of the twelve Prime Ministers 1721–70 was four years one month whereas that of the twelve from 1834 to 1908 was six years two months. That of the most recent twelve is down to five years. One can perhaps say that very long periods in office seem to have gone. Salisbury, the last Prime Minister to reach double figures, retired in 1902. Since then the longest have been Asquith and Churchill, each with eight years eight months. But I wrote those words before the results of the election of October 1974. A recent correspondent to *The Times* tells us that Mr. Wilson will beat them both if he is still in office on 4 March 1977. If he can stay one year and four months longer, to the

end of July 1978 he will have achieved double figures—
the first to have done so since Lord Salisbury.

Now let us look at their educational background. Only
four did not go to school at all and were brought up by
private tutors. The most famous is the younger Pitt. Eton,
as one would expect, because of its long ascendancy as
a seminary for the upper class, accounts for much the
largest number—twenty. Harrow is next with seven followed by Westminster with six. The only other school to
boast of more than one is, oddly enough, Glasgow High
School with two—Campbell-Bannerman and Bonar Law.
Their success at school varied greatly. Some, like Peel and
Gladstone, were very much at the top of the class. Others
like Baldwin went by unnoticed. I cannot find that any
was actually expelled, but I may be wrong.

Only ten out of our forty-nine did not have a university
education. Twenty-four went to Oxford, fourteen to Cambridge, two to Edinburgh, and two to Glasgow, but of those
who attended Scottish universities, three went on to an
Oxford or Cambridge college subsequently. The ascendancy
of Oxford and Cambridge combined is not surprising, but
I have never seen a convincing explanation of the relative
predominance of Oxford. Whatever the reason, the balance
has remained much the same over the years, with latterly
an even more marked bias. The score was eight–five in
the eighteenth century, nine–six in the nineteenth, and
is so far seven–three in the twentieth. The last six Prime
Ministers have been Oxford men. It would be interesting
to know whether an analysis of the political world in
general—Cabinets, House of Commons, House of Lords
would reveal a similar preponderance, but the task would
be lengthy and luckily lies outside my terms of reference.

Of colleges in either university Christ Church has an
overwhelming lead with fourteen.[1] Trinity, Cambridge, is

---

[1] Counting Lord Bath. Thirteen is the usual number given.

B

next with five and St. John's, Cambridge with four. The most frequent school/university combination is Eton and Christ Church, which with ten accounts for just over one-fifth of all Prime Ministers. It is perhaps a testimony to the tenacity of the British governing class that this combination, the very symbol of traditional aristocratic background, should have been represented by two Prime Ministers within the last twenty years, Anthony Eden (1955-7) and Sir Alec Douglas-Home (1963-4). However, they did not have the lengthy tenure of Gladstone and Salisbury whose education was the same—and perhaps that signifies something or other.

To come into the premiership with no experience of cabinet office is rare. I can only find five cases and three of them, the Dukes of Devonshire and Portland and Earl Waldegrave, really date from a period when it is hard to discern a Cabinet at all. Of the other two Addington was Speaker, and Ramsay MacDonald headed a new party. Thirty-seven Prime Ministers have been Secretaries of State either for Home or Foreign Affairs (or before 1782 of the Northern or Southern Departments) or Chancellors of the Exchequer—in some cases holding more than one of these offices on their way to the premiership. The remaining seven, Wellington, Derby, Balfour, Campbell-Bannerman, Attlee, Wilson, and Heath, all had experience of office in scarcely less important, though less prestigious, positions. No Lord Chancellor has ever become Prime Minister, nor has any Viceroy of India. There has, however, been at least one Lord Lieutenant of Ireland.

More Prime Ministers than one might think have taken a humbler post after ceasing to be at the head. 'Caesar could hardly have led a legion under Pompey,' Trollope makes the Duke of Omnium say, but his mentor, the old Duke of St. Bungay, replies, 'It has been done greatly to the service of the country and without the slightest loss of honour to him that did it'. In the twentieth century one can think of Sir Alec Douglas-Home, Neville Chamberlain, Stanley Baldwin, Ramsay MacDonald, and A. J. Balfour; and, going further back, Russell, Wellington, Goderich, Addington, and Portland.

Age of entry into office, tenure of office, school, university —can one construct a sort of 'mean' or 'average' Prime Minister, or, as perhaps would be a better expression, a Highest Common Factor of a Prime Minister? Yes, one can. The answer is the Duke of Portland (April–December 1783 and March 1807–October 1809). He was at Eton and Christ Church. He held office for more than three and less than four years—the most frequent tenure, and he entered it at 46 for the first time—over 45 and under 50 which is the most frequent quinquennium or lustre in which people have been appointed.

However interesting this exercise may be, it does not prove much. No one at the word Prime Minister would have a sort of word association or Pavlovian response 'Duke of Portland'. In any case there are other criteria. Dukes (five) are, as one would expect, a minority among Prime Ministers though not such a minority as the lowest grade of the United Kingdom peerage, or the Scottish Representative peerage, or the Irish peerage or the baronetage each of which can only claim one.

The most frequent rank to be found among peer Prime Ministers is that of earl (ten); and this does not include three who became earls in midstream and one who renounced his earldom as a necessary preliminary to putting into the water. Nor of course does it include the numerous Prime Ministers who were made earls after leaving office as a recognition of their services.

The precedent of an earldom as a reward for a Prime Minister was set by the creation of Sir Robert Walpole as Earl of Orford, but like the Garter there seems to have been 'no damned merit about it', for a very dim Prime Minister like Goderich was also made an earl in due course. If, however, a man was already an earl it was not usually deemed necessary to raise his rank. It is true that Queen Victoria offered to confer dukedoms on the Earl of Derby and the Earl of Beaconsfield but both of them refused. Since the 'spirit of the age' nowadays seems to be against hereditary titles, presumably the Earl of Avon will be the last example of the traditional earldom—unless the Life Peerages Act is amended to allow grades other than barons to be created under its provisions. (I rather like the idea of life earls, marquesses, and dukes.)

Between Walpole's accession and the Parliament Act of 1911, no less than twenty Prime Ministers were in the Upper House for all their time compared with fourteen who were in the Commons throughout. (Of the twenty peers only six never sat at all in the House of Commons.) Yet, even if we add in the three who moved into the Lords before retiring, the total period during which Britain was governed by a peer was only 70 years out of 190.

This is perhaps not very surprising. The House of Commons undoubtedly became the dominant branch long before the Parliament Act formally confirmed the fact. What is much more surprising is the chronology. Most constitutional historians would regard the House of Lords as far nearer to being a co-equal branch of the legislature in the eighteenth century than in the nineteenth century. The defeat of the Fox–North Coalition in the House of Lords meant the fall of the Government. But successive Reform Acts gave the Commons an authority and legitimacy as a representative body, which it could be argued not to possess in the heyday of eighteenth-century corruption—the era of Old Sarum, etc. By the 1820s the House of Lords was under heavy fire from radical opinion as an antiquated abuse, and in the full flood of reformist zeal during the 1830s few people would have predicted a long life for such a strangely anomalous institution. It was the Lower House alone which now made and unmade governments, and a defeat in the House of Lords was regarded as a minor annoyance. Yet during the eighty years of the eighteenth century following Walpole's accession the Prime Minister was in the House of Lords for less than a sixth of the time (just under thirteen years); whereas during the next century there was a peer as Prime Minister for fifty-five years—over half the time. I suspect that the status, authority, and procedure of the nineteenth-century House of Lords would repay a much closer study than it has received from constitutional historians.

Although the last Prime Minister to sit in the House of Lords—Lord Salisbury—retired in 1902, the possibility of a repetition was by no means ruled out. There was a determined effort by a group of Liberals (the party least favourable to the Lords) to elevate Campbell-Bannerman as a peer Prime Minister in 1905. Their motives were anything but disinterested and Campbell-Bannerman refused. Nevertheless, the episode showed that a Prime Minister in the Upper House could not yet be regarded as out of the question. Even after the passage of the Parliament Act such an appointment was still considered feasible. When Balfour retired from the leadership of the Conservative party in the autumn of 1911, Bonar Law succeeded to only a part of the inheritance, the lead in the Commons. Lord Lansdowne remained leader of the Lords, and in accordance with past precedent (e.g. Sir Stafford Northcote and Lord Salisbury from 1881 to 1885) there was no leader of the party as a whole. If the Liberals had been ousted, as they might have been, over the Irish crisis of 1912–14, it was by no means certain that the Crown's choice would fall on Law. It could equally well —perhaps more probably—have fallen on Lansdowne.

The succession of Baldwin rather than Curzon in 1923 has often been cited as an example of the effect of the Parliament Act, and more generally the impossibility of a peer as Prime Minister. But the very full examination which has now been made by various historians into that highly controversial crisis shows that it was only a part of the reason and not in itself conclusive. When yet another crisis arose, following the ambiguous result of the general election of 1923, among many names canvassed as possible Prime Ministers of a Conservative–Liberal coalition were those of Lord Balfour and Lord Derby. As late as 1940 it seemed well within the bounds of possibility that Lord Halifax would become Prime Minister. Chamberlain would have preferred him to Churchill. More surprisingly, so would the Labour party. It did not come off for Halifax withdrew his claim, but it was very far from being ruled out absolutely *en principe*.

But of one thing we can be sure. It is no longer possible now for a peer to be Prime Minister. If proof is needed it is in the events of 1963 when Mr. Macmillan's—happily temporary—collapse of health necessitated his resignation just at the moment of a Conservative Party Conference in Blackpool. By a curious chance the Peerage Renunciation Act had recently become law and the period of grace during which existing peers had to make up their minds what to do had not yet expired. The fourteenth Earl of Home and the second Viscount Hailsham decided to doff their coronets, but, such are the strange vicissitudes of fortune, their coronets are now back on their heads once again, albeit in the attenuated form worn by a mere baron.

The wealth of Prime Ministers has varied enormously. It would be wrong to speculate, for it can only be speculation, on the position of living persons. Excluding them, I would guess that the richest of all was the fourteenth Earl of Derby who had a rent roll of £100,000 p.a. in the eighteen-fifties, with Lord Rosebery as runner-up. But some of the eighteenth-century dukes, with Portland at the top of the list, must also have been very wealthy. Few Prime Ministers have made much money. Mr. A. J. P. Taylor says of Lloyd George that he was the first Prime Minister since Walpole to 'leave office flagrantly richer than he entered it', adding for good measure that he was also 'the first since the Duke of Grafton to live openly with his mistress'.[1]

The sexual morals of Prime Ministers have also varied considerably. Melbourne is the only one to have been cited in the then equivalent of a divorce suit. He was acquitted, but the family seem to have been sceptical. 'Do not let William think himself invulnerable for having got off again this time',[2] wrote his brother to their sister, 'No man's luck can go further.' Palmerston's amours as a young man were famous. By the time he was Prime Minister he had become 'respectable'. Gladstone declared that most of the Prime Ministers he had known had been adulterers. I daresay, without being unduly cynical, that in this respect Prime Ministers have not diverged much from the morals of the social class to which they belonged at the particular time in which they lived.

What was that social class? The class structure in England at any period we wish to consider is peculiarly complicated and difficult to explain. Is there such a thing as 'the governing class'? What do we mean by the aristocracy, the squirearchy, the middle class—or for that matter the working class? There is, I suppose, a logic-chopping sense in which one could say that all Prime Ministers belonged to the 'governing class', for by definition they govern. Common sense needs to be invoked here. Obviously Ramsay MacDonald did not belong to the same

[1] *English History 1914–1945* (1965), p. 74.
[2] Quoted, Lord David Cecil, *Lord M* (1954), p. 165.

class as Baldwin. Nor did Baldwin belong to the same class
as his rival for the Tory succession in 1923, Lord Curzon.

I prefer to look at it in terms of 'outsiders' and 'insiders'.
There is at any moment of time a class of society from
which one might expect a Prime Minister to be drawn and
one from which one would not. The very fact that there
is contemporary comment in this sense is an indication.
When she appointed Disraeli Queen Victoria wrote to her
daughter, 'a proud thing for a Man "risen from the people"
to have obtained'.[1] Disraeli had not of course risen from
the people in the ordinary sense of the word. His father
had been a comfortably off rentier-cum-literary man living
in a beautiful red-brick Queen Anne country-house at
Bradenham. What the Queen meant—and she was right—
was that Disraeli came from a class, group, background,
which did not normally produce Prime Ministers at that
particular period of time. Obviously someone with an
outsider's background at one period would not be similarly
regarded at another. Neither Mr. Wilson nor Mr. Heath
are 'outsiders'. But Addington, son of a doctor, Canning,
son of an actress, and Peel, son of a self-made cotton
millionaire had elements of the outsider about them despite
their conventional education. In a much later period something of the same could be said of Bonar Law. But the
quintessential 'outsiders' are Disraeli, Lloyd George, and
Ramsay MacDonald. There has been no one comparable
to any of them since. If Ernest Bevin had become Prime
Minister he would certainly have qualified, but he never
even wished to challenge that 'insider', Clement Attlee.

The intellectual and oratorical powers of Prime Ministers
have greatly varied but none of them has been totally dull
or entirely incoherent. Some have been poor speakers like
the Duke of Portland, Lord Aberdeen, and Campbell-
Bannerman. Some have contrived to be faintly ridiculous,

[1] Quoted from Royal Archives, Robert Blake, *Disraeli* (1966), p. 487.

like the Duke of Newcastle and Addington. It has suited some to appear considerably less intelligent than they actually were—Palmerston, Baldwin, and Sir Alec Douglas-Home are examples. But even those very few Prime Ministers who showed themselves palpably unfit for office —and by this I do not mean just unsuccessful ones—have rarely been stupid. I suppose the six Prime Ministers who really were unsuited to the post and who should never have allowed themselves to accept were Bute who was merely a court favourite; the Duke of Grafton whose moral conduct was not redeemed by royal descent or the power to manage men; Shelburne whom no one trusted; Goderich who was always bursting into tears and never even met Parliament—said to be the original of Hilaire Belloc's Lord Lundy; Aberdeen who drifted into the Crimean War; Rosebery who for all his gifts simply could not endure the compromises and accommodations that even the strongest Prime Minister must make if he is to survive. None of these were dullards and two of them were very clever. None was incompetent in administration or debate. They had held important offices before they reached the top. (Indeed, people are not regarded as runners at all without good reason.) But they did not have the Prime Ministerial temperament—that mysterious entity so wonderfully analysed by Trollope in his great political novel about the Duke who lacked it.

To define that temperament would not be easy. Courage, tenacity, determination, firm nerves, and clarity of mind are some of the qualities. So, too, are a certain toughness of the skin and a certain insensitivity, or at least the lack of great sensitivity. Nor should a Prime Minister be worried too much by scruples and doubts. And if tact and the power to manage men are there too, so much the better. No doubt few Prime Ministers have had every one of these virtues, but if they have not had most of them they have not got very far. Possession of the right temperament is not a guarantee of success, but lack of it is a firm guarantee of failure.

Prime Ministers are not usually men of original mind. There are exceptions. Lloyd George and Churchill might be thus described—and perhaps Disraeli. It was no accident that only the convulsion of war and a critical juncture in the affairs of the nation brought the first two to the top. As for Disraeli he got there despite, not because of, his ideas. But in general Bagehot's famous description of Peel in whom he saw the essential virtues of the parliamentary statesman holds good, even though it was written in the placid heyday of Victorian England's supremacy, 'the powers of a first rate man, the creed of a second rate man'; or as he puts it elsewhere 'a man of common opinions and uncommon abilities'. The truth is that originality is mistrusted in politics and a man with original ideas finds it hard to climb unless he keeps them to himself.

I suppose that what fascinates one about the personalities is the endless adventure and the elements of chance. Some few were pre-ordained for the post. The younger Pitt was one, Peel another, the Earl of Derby a third. Gladstone from his early parliamentary days onward would have been a good bet. Likewise Canning, Russell, and Eden. But think of the odd series of events which put Disraeli into Number Ten; or which elevated Campbell-Bannerman at the age of 69, known as one of the laziest men in politics—'I am a great believer in the horizontal position', he once said —with his highest ambition as the Speakership; or the chance that made Bonar Law Prime Minister, as the result of a deadlocked party election eleven years earlier, from which the two main contestants withdrew. (Who can say whether some similar contest may not, in no less chancy a way, produce another unpredictable Prime Minister?) If Bonar Law's health had not collapsed when it did, before

Austen Chamberlain and the Coalition Conservatives had become reconciled with the main body of the party, if Balfour had not detested Curzon, or if there had been no conspiracy by J. C. C. Davidson and Colonel Waterhouse,[1] Baldwin might never have reached the top. In the event he did. He dominated the inter-war years which have been described—not fancifully—as 'the Baldwin Era'. But by how very narrow a margin it could all have gone so differently.

These contrasts in age, circumstances, and chance make one reluctant to generalize about the qualities needed for a Prime Minister. I have suggested half a dozen who were so unsuited by temperament to the job that they should never have taken it. Some might add further names to that list. I would like to end by suggesting at the other end of the scale the 'great' prime ministers. There seem to me to be seven who qualify: in the eighteenth century, Walpole, Chatham, and the younger Pitt; in the nineteenth, Peel and Gladstone (not, I think, Disraeli who was a great character but not a great Prime Minister, nor Palmerston nor Salisbury who were, however, great Foreign Secretaries); and in the twentieth century, Lloyd George and Winston Churchill. Others might be added to the list but I doubt whether anyone would wish to subtract. To all of them Bagehot's observation applies.

The Prime Minister is at the head of our business [he writes] and like every head of a business he ought to have mind in reserve. He must be able to take a fresh view of new contingencies and keep an animated curiosity as to coming events. If he suffer himself to be involved in minutiae, some great change in the world, some Franco-German war may break out, like a thief in the night, and if he has no elastic thought and no

---

[1] Cameron Hazlehurst, 'The Baldwinite Conspiracy', *Historical Studies* (University of Melbourne), vol. 16, no. 63, October 1974, pp. 167–91 reveals the full measure of these activities for the first time.

spare energy he may make the worst errors. A great Premier must add the vivacity of a lazy man to the assiduity of a very laborious one.[1]

This seems to me as true as when it was written a hundred years ago. It may not be a guarantee of greatness but no Prime Minister will be great or even merely success-ful if he does not have that mixture of qualities.

[1] Norman St. John Stevas (ed.), *The Collected Works of Walter Bagehot*, vi (1974), p. 67.

II. THE HISTORY

I WANT to discuss in this lecture the development of the office of Prime Minister from Walpole to the accession of Lloyd George at the end of 1916. As I said in my previous lecture, the position of a Prime Minister in the reigns of George I and George II was in many respects very different from his position today. It was also very different from his position in the later years of George III. Moreover, the state of affairs at the end of the eighteenth century under, say, Pitt or Addington was not at all the same as it was to be under Peel; and the office under Peel was not the same as it was to be under Balfour or Asquith. I have already given some arguments for adhering to the traditional view that Walpole was the first Prime Minister. This is defensible, if only on the grounds that by the time he departed in 1742 there had been changes in the nature of the office held by the King's principal minister so substantial as to justify a new description. It would, however, be wrong to go a step further and call him, as some have done, the first *modern* Prime Minister. If that title can be given intelligibly to any single person it is certainly not to Walpole, nor even the younger Pitt. I doubt whether any Prime Minister before Peel would qualify.

Walpole's position differed in three crucial respects. First he depended not only for his appointment but also for his continuance in office upon the favour of the King. It is true that Walpole had shown by the end of his career that the First Minister could not survive unless he could manage Parliament, indeed that determined opposition in the House of Commons would make his continuance impossible whatever the will of the King. Lord North, on the verge of resignation, put the point clearly forty years later to George III. 'Your Majesty is well apprized that in this country [North was presumably contrasting it with Hanover] the Prince on the Throne cannot with prudence oppose the deliberate resolution of the House of Commons.'[1] It was not of course that the House could—or claimed to— choose a particular Prime Minister, let alone a particular ministry. Its power was negative. One could almost compare it with that recently exercised by the major trade unions—the ability to stop a government they dislike, not —or not yet—to nominate one that they like. It was reluctantly recognized, rather than constitutionally accepted —a disagreeable fact of life rather than an approved usage. The power of the House in this respect was seldom exercised. Normally the House could be 'managed' by the First Minister, as Walpole and Pelham and North himself had done for many years, and as Pitt was to do too from 1784 onwards. It was when a crisis arose, when management no longer worked, that this reserve power came into effect. The King still possessed great authority. Even if he had to find someone who could manage Parliament, and had to get rid of someone who could not, the fact remained that he had a wide freedom of choice. There was unlikely to be only a single person at any one time who could perform this function. The situation was made clear enough by the recognized precariousness of Walpole's position when George I died. George II could well have dismissed him and many people including Walpole himself expected this to happen. Walpole would not have complained on constitutional grounds if it had.

Secondly the King was himself an active executive figure who took part in the process of government. If there is any analogy today, the relationship of the Prime Minister with

[1] John Brooke, *King George III* (1972), p. 222.

the monarch was not unlike that of the French Prime Minister with the President of France under the constitution of the Fifth Republic. The King was, if anything, more powerful. The French Prime Minister does at least make up his own Cabinet and present it to the President. The monarch in the earlier part of the eighteenth century actually appointed the key officers of state himself and not simply on the advice of the Prime Minister. Of course there was a certain element of give and take, and Walpole did contrive from time to time to get rid of the more disagreeable colleagues thrust upon him. But he had to do so by argument and tact; he could not give 'advice' which was binding. Indeed as Sir Edgar Williams points out in his well-known article on the Cabinet in the eighteenth century:

> To suggest—and it has been done very often—that the King was bound to accept the advice of the ministers whom he had chosen, whose tenure was during his good pleasure and whose majority in the House was conditioned by his patronage is . . . preposterous.[1]

From this followed a third important difference. Ministers did not go out *en bloc* just because the Prime Minister resigned or was dismissed. Their loyalty was not to him but to the Crown. As I mentioned before, we do not get a complete change of ministers with the departure of the Prime Minister until 1782 when Rockingham succeeded Lord North. A Prime Minister who cannot automatically carry his colleagues out with him is obviously in a very different position from one who can—and a much weaker position.

The one point of continuity throughout the whole period we are considering is the need for the First Minister

---

[1] E. T. Williams, 'The Cabinet in the Eighteenth Century', *History*, xxii (1937). This is one of the most important articles on the subject and I acknowledge my debt to it for much of what follows.

to be able to control the House of Commons. No doubt in the eighteenth, and for a part of the nineteenth century too, he had to have the confidence of the King. But royal confidence was never enough in itself, and, although the King by entrusting his powers of patronage to the First Lord of the Treasury virtually guaranteed the results of general elections, he could not be sure that the minister of his choice would retain control over the House *between* general elections. To control the House of Commons is much easier if you belong to it, especially if you double the post of Chancellor of the Exchequer, as was almost invariably done by commoner Prime Ministers from Walpole to Peel (the elder Pitt of course breaks all the rules). This explains the far greater longevity in office of commoners than peers during the eighteenth century—Walpole, Pelham, Lord North, the younger Pitt. What is less easy, as I said before, is to explain why, in the nineteenth century, membership of the Commons became less important and why peers had no particular difficulty in holding the premiership—Liverpool, Grey, Melbourne, Derby, Salisbury.

The first major change in the position of the Prime Minister as created and defined by Walpole occurred under the pressure of war; such changes very often do. The Seven Years War made it essential to have a single man in charge—a directing and dominant personality. The elder Pitt controlled events in a way which Walpole had never quite done, but with the end of the war the old system returned. Government was again carried on by departments under the King, and the Prime Minister tended to be a chairman rather than an executive—a sort of liaison figure between the Crown and the Commons, not a driving force in the affairs of the country. Lord North's twelve-year administration embodied all these features, and its disastrous consequences were part of the reason why the system changed once again after his eclipse, and this time changed irreversibly.

The circumstances in which the younger Pitt entered office constituted a crisis of confidence. In an article in *The Times* of 30 September 1974 Mr. Ian Bradley compared the circumstances of 1782–4 with those of today. No historical analogy should be pressed too far, but the resemblances are certainly striking—loss of empire (the American colonies), trouble in Ireland, economic depression, breakdown of law and order (the Gordon Riots), and disillusionment with the whole governmental system. The country needed a new man. Here the resemblance ceases, for in 1783 a new leader was forthcoming in the person of the younger Pitt. He dominated the political scene for over twenty-two years, and he left a lasting imprint on the office of Prime Minister.

The illness of George III was one of the reasons of change. It was by then mentally and physically impossible for the King to take the active part played by his predecessors. Another change scarcely obvious at the time—but these changes never are—was the altered status of what is called the 'efficient Cabinet'. There has been a long debate about the origins of the modern cabinet and it is no part of my theme to go into this very complicated subject in any detail. The writings of Professor Aspinall, Sir Edgar Williams, Professor Plumb, and others have disentangled the historical knot in so far as it can be. All that need be said for the purpose of this survey is that the Cabinet Council (from an inner group of which the Cabinet, as we know it, is descended) lost the residue of its diminishing influence, and the *conciliabulum* or 'efficient Cabinet' replaced it entirely.

The 'sole' or First Minister was better situated to control the 'efficient Cabinet' than the Cabinet Council which might contain people who were not chosen by him, not

c

in his confidence, not even on his side politically. They
might be 'spies' for the King when the King had to deal
with a ministry which he regarded as thrust upon him.
It was this body, not the 'efficient Cabinet', over which
George II occasionally presided. Even George III did so
on two occasions, in 1779 and 1781—though by then the
practice had become so unusual that it evoked comment.
In the earlier part of the eighteenth century the Cabinet
Council, in addition to the members of the 'efficient
Cabinet' such as the First Lord of the Treasury, Secretaries
of State, Lord Chancellor, and Lord President, contained
at various times the Archbishop of Canterbury, the Lord
Chief Justice, great court officials like the Lord Chamberlain and the Lord High Steward, also the Commander-in-
Chief and one or two more people, usually peers, chosen
for their general standing and prestige. As Sir Lewis
Namier puts it, they were a Council of State rather than
an Administration. By the time George III came to the
throne the Cabinet Council had almost fallen into desue-
tude, and seemed to be used only to hear the King's
speech and to advise the King on death sentences. Hence
Lord Temple's reference in July 1766 to it as 'the hanging
Committee'. Yet it lingered on. George III was prepared
to play off the Council against the *conciliabulum*—rarely
and not very successfully, it is true, but the attempt was
made. The last flicker was Lord Loughborough's effort to
remain a member of the 'efficient Cabinet' in 1801 after
he had resigned the Great Seal and had been replaced
by Lord Eldon. He turned up uninvited at meetings of
Addington's Cabinet. He would have had a good claim
to be a member of the Cabinet Council, but the new Prime
Minister felt obliged to point out after ten days that although,
as he put it in the stately language of the day, 'personally
gratified in having the benefit of your Lordship's counsell
and assistance' he none the less took the view 'that the

members of the Cabinet should not exceed that of persons whose responsible situations in office require their being members of it'. And he ended 'I hope your Lordship will give me full credit for the motives by which I can alone be actuated upon this occasion, as well as for the sincere sentiments of esteem and regard with which I am, my dear Lord, your Lordship's most obedient and faithful servant, Henry Addington'.[1]

Whether this consoled Lord Loughborough is perhaps doubtful. He was not the first or last of those Lord Chancellors and others immortalized by Raymond Asquith in his *Lines to a Statesman*:

> He left the high affairs of state
> For Aeschylus and Livy.
> He hurled the Great Seal in the grate
> And the Privy Seal in the privy.

The episode formalized what had probably been the usage for twenty years past. The 'efficient Cabinet' was the government, and it was now the Prime Minister's government, even under a relative nonentity like Addington scarcely remembered but for Canning's witty couplet. The 'nominal Cabinet' or 'Cabinet Council' fades from history. Sir Lewis Namier in an enjoyable essay[2] dates its final disappearance at a decision made in July 1921 that the King's Speech which in February of that year had been read to a 'Cabinet Council attenuated and atrophied' should be sent instead to Balmoral in a box.

But this is a digression. The point about the disappearance of the 'nominal Cabinet' is that it removed an institution through which, in however shadowy a way, the Crown could in some measure operate against the Prime

[1] Lord Campbell, *Lives of the Lord Chancellors*, vi (1847), p. 327.
[2] Lewis Namier, *In the Margin of History* (1939), pp. 105–14.

Minister. The position of the Prime Minister was thus strengthened and the change contributed to the long ascendancy of the younger Pitt. A corollary was limitation of the Cabinet to what Addington called 'persons whose responsible situation requires them being members of it'. This did not preclude membership of some who held sinecure offices such as the Privy Seal or the Lord Presidency, but it did mean that the key members were ministers with an active job to do.

Pitt's administration did not see the disappearance of royal power. His position may have been stronger *vis-à-vis* the Crown than that of Walpole or Pelham or North, but it was not as strong as that of Peel would be. The Crown was still a force in politics as far as appointments were concerned, even though the King gradually ceased to interfere in day-to-day policy. Partly through illness, partly through the disappearance of the 'nominal Cabinet', partly through the growth of an embryonic party system such as had not existed at the beginning of his reign, he became more remote from what modern jargon calls 'the decision-making process'. This removal of the Crown from an active role in the formation of policy enhanced the importance of the Prime Minister. In 1803, out of office, Pitt told Lord Melville that it was 'an absolute necessity . . . that there should be an avowed and real Minister possessing the chief weight in the Council and the principal place in the confidence of the King'.[1]

A corollary of this was what we now call the collective responsibility of the Cabinet. That question came up in 1792 when Lord Chancellor Thurlow violently attacked Pitt's Sinking Fund in the House of Lords, although he had not raised the slightest objection to it in the Cabinet. The Prime Minister promptly got rid of him but the method is interestingly indicative of the still powerful role of the

[1] Stanhope, *Pitt*, iv (1862), p. 24, quoted Williams, op. cit., p. 20.

Crown in the matter of appointments if not of policy. Pitt wrote to Thurlow thus:[1]

My Lord

I think it right to take the earliest opportunity of acquainting your Lordship, that being convinced of the impossibility of his Majesty's service being any longer carried on to advantage while your Lordship and myself both remain in our present situations, I have felt it my duty to submit that opinion to his Majesty; humbly requesting his Majesty's determination thereupon.

I have the honour to be etc.

W. Pitt

The King confronted with this choice called for the return of the Great Seal much to the Lord Chancellor's surprise and mortification. From then onwards it was no longer possible except by some special agreement for a member of the Cabinet to disagree publicly with one of its measures. He had to support it or go. Melbourne's celebrated doctrine about it not mattering what we say as long as we all say the same thing had already arrived.

Pitt was not a believer in putting too many things to his 'efficient Cabinet'. What Prime Minister ever is? Most of them prefer to keep much to themselves and to play their cards close to their chests. Pitt would discuss matters with Dundas or his Grenville cousin. He would come to the Cabinet with his decision settled although he would tactfully listen to his colleagues before he announced it. On at least one occasion, as Professor Aspinall has discovered, he wrote the minutes before the meeting. The change which occurred during Pitt's long tenure was never reversed. Far less dominant figures than he, Addington, Grenville, Perceval, Liverpool, inherited a position of much more power than that of Pitt's predecessors. But the modern premiership had not arrived yet. On one

[1] Campbell, op. cit., v, p. 604.

important matter the Prime Minister remained in a very different situation from his successors after 1832. His appointment depended on the King who was still in a real sense the head of the executive, and in the end his control over the House of Commons depended partly, though never wholly, on his exercise in his capacity as First Lord of the Treasury of the patronage delegated to him by the Crown. And the King could dismiss him.

This in effect was what happened in 1801 over Catholic Emancipation when Pitt proposed a policy which the King could not reconcile with his conscience or his coronation oath. It was Pitt who had to give way, not the King, and there was a repetition of the same conflict in 1807. Pitt's resignation in favour of Addington, Grenville's in favour of Portland, are striking illustrations of the residual power of the Crown. The King could still, despite all the changes in the balance of the constitution, remove a Prime Minister whose policy he disliked. The Napoleonic wars had in many ways enhanced the position of the Prime Minister. The King, even a King in good health, was simply incapable of coping with the immense extra burden imposed by wartime needs. Nevertheless he had the last word—and was regarded as rightly having the last word—over the appointment and dismissal of 'the Minister'.

The same question came up from November 1810 onwards when George III finally went mad. The Prince Regent, though restricted for a year by the Regency Act from exercising the full powers of a king, was regarded as having an indisputable constitutional right to dismiss Spencer Perceval and appoint a new Prime Minister. By February 1812 his powers were entirely untrammelled. In fact, to the wrath of his old Foxite friends, he made no change, but no one would have cavilled at his constitutional right to do so.

The Prime Minister did indeed vanish from the scene,

murdered in the lobby of the House of Commons by a
madman. Once again the Foxites had high hopes but the
upshot of this fresh ministerial crisis was a continuation
of the same group under the leadership of Lord Liverpool
—by posterity one of the most underrated of all our Prime
Ministers, thanks largely to the mordant caricature drawn
by Disraeli who had his own reasons for putting across
this travesty of history. The status of the Prime Minister
achieved by the eighteen years of William Pitt's rule was
consolidated by the fourteen years during which Lord
Liverpool was in office. But he too had to reckon with
the Crown. George IV tried in 1820 to substitute Addington
(Lord Sidmouth) who refused from personal loyalty—but
not from any feeling of constitutional impropriety. A year
later the King effectively vetoed the admission of Canning
to the Cabinet. In 1822, after Castlereagh's death, he
offered the leadership in the House of Commons and the
Chancellorship of the Exchequer to Peel who declined.
In that same year the King did at last, under strong
pressure, agree to accept Canning whom he then came
to respect and admire. When Liverpool was incapacitated
early in 1827 by a stroke from which he never recovered
George IV's choice fell on Canning. There was a curious
episode, however, during the interregnum when the King,
aware of the dissensions in the Administration, suggested
that the Cabinet like a board of directors which elects its
own chairman should choose the Prime Minister. Peel
objected on principle to this delegation of royal authority.
It would have been an interesting constitutional precedent
if it had been adopted, and the list of Prime Ministers from
1827 onwards might well have been different. When
Canning died, Lord Goderich was very much the King's
choice—and a bad one at that.

The death of George IV in 1830, the accession of his
brother, the consequent general election, and the train

of events resulting in the Reform Act of 1832 constitute the biggest change in the whole history of the office of Prime Minister—the change from the concept of government as the King's government to that of government as party government. Lord Liverpool, the Duke of Wellington, Lord Grey, even Lord Melbourne under whom the final symbolic change occurred, in so far as they reflected on the matter at all would have thought of themselves primarily as servants of the Crown—and of course there is a sense in which Prime Ministers still—and quite rightly —think of themselves in that light today. The difference is that until 1832 the Crown could within certain limits choose a Prime Minister who would be sure to win an ensuing general election. This was because of the 'influence' which automatically went to him by virtue of his position as First Lord of the Treasury. It is significant that from 1715 to 1835 no government actually lost a general election. Even in 1830 Wellington was not defeated at the polls. He lost his position by subsequent mismanagement. In such a situation, although the Prime Minister had to be able to control Parliament and was liable to be pushed out if he was palpably incompetent to do so, it was no less vital for him to manage the monarch.

All this was changed—though not immediately—with the events of 1834–5. In November 1834 the death of Earl Spencer and the succession of his son, Lord Althorp, to the peerage created a vacancy in the leadership of the House of Commons. Rather than accept the nomination of Lord John Russell, William IV dismissed Melbourne, making the same interpretation of his own constitutional role that his father had made when dismissing the Fox–North Coalition half a century earlier. He assumed that Peel, after an interval in which to collect his forces together, would dissolve, and win the next general election even as the younger Pitt had done in 1784. But events did not work out that way, nor did Wellington, or Peel who took office with reluctance, expect them to do so. The world of 1834 was very different from that of 1784, and not only because of the Reform Act. For many years past 'royal government' had been running down. By the 1820s there were signs that the supply of patronage—the oil that greased the moving parts of the old machine— was beginning to be insufficient. Successive Tory govern- ments in 1818, 1820, 1826, and 1830 managed to win the elections but with increasing difficulty. The general election of January 1835, however, saw the first clear decision against a Prime Minister who had the avowed support of the King. Peel tried to carry on, but the Whigs were determined to force him out. After numerous defeats he resigned in April. The King was obliged to send for Melbourne and to accept Lord John Russell as Leader of the House. It was by the old standards a humiliating rebuff. The King was so angry that he declared that he would not ask his new ministers to dinner, but they carried on un- perturbed (possibly even relieved) by this threat.

Never again was a monarch to dismiss a Prime Minister, although some monarchs continued to talk as if they could, and in the Ulster crisis of 1912–14 such a course was urged on George V by the hotter-headed Unionists. But when once it was clear that the Crown could no longer ensure electoral success for its own nominee there was really no choice between the risk of open political partisanship which the Crown could not in the end survive and with- drawal to the position of neutrality which prevails today.

Yet the logic of the situation was not at once apparent. The Bedchamber Crisis of May 1839 is one example. Neither Peel nor Melbourne would have behaved quite as they did if the Crown had been regarded as a neutral factor in politics, and the situation was made no easier by Mel- bourne's dual role as Prime Minister and Queen's Private

Secretary—a combination which was ended soon after her marriage to Prince Albert who took on that task himself. As late as 1841 the Prince was horrified to find that money from the Privy Purse had been used towards Whig expenses in the general election of that year. The Queen was, moreover, still sufficiently imbued with the notion that the government were 'her' servants to declare privately that she would not have agreed to the dissolution if she had expected Melbourne to lose.

Although the 1830s were marked by this important change from Crown government to party government, it would be a mistake to think that it was the sort of party government which we know today. The Prime Minister did, it is true, have to keep his party behind him if he was to survive, as Peel found to his cost in 1846. But parties were not the cohesive all-embracing organizations familiar to us. They were ill-disciplined groups, each with a fringe of those independent members whom Disraeli described as members who could not be depended upon. If power had passed from the Crown it had not yet moved to the electorate. In fact the period from 1835 to 1868 saw the heyday of the supremacy of the House of Commons— the situation so brilliantly described by Bagehot at the very moment that it was on the verge of being transformed into something quite different. The Cabinet may not have been, as he claimed, a committee of the legislature, but it was the House of Commons rather than the electorate which made and unmade governments. Six parliaments were elected between 1841 and 1868; and in all six of them the House of Commons had brought down at least one administration, and sometimes two, before its dissolution.

Nor did the Prime Minister possess the full authority that he came to have later. A good example is the right to dismiss a minister. Writing as late as 1877 Salisbury reassured Carnarvon who was wondering whether Disraeli intended to dismiss them both. There had, he said, been no example of such action since Pitt dismissed Thurlow in 1792. He thought it was virtually impossible for a Prime Minister to do it without a strong reason publicly defensible. He did not mention the case of Russell and Palmerston in 1851, but in one sense it tended to confirm Salisbury's view, for Russell only took the final step with great reluctance, after much provocation, and great pressure from the Queen and the Prince—and there was a strongly defensible reason for his action. Palmerston had, on any view, behaved outrageously.

Early in 1884 Gladstone wanted to remove Lord Carlingford, the Lord Privy Seal, in order to make a place for Lord Rosebery. There was nothing against Carlingford and he would not resign. Gladstone was most reluctant to dismiss him. 'Mr. Gladstone', wrote Harcourt to Morley, 'entertains great doubts as to the right of a Prime Minister to require a Cabinet Minister to resign.' In fact Carlingford stayed on till the end of the year when he did at last go of his own accord.

One may perhaps see in these attitudes something of a carry-over from the different conventions prevailing in the years between the Reform Acts of 1832 and 1867. Disraeli, Gladstone, and Salisbury had started their political careers then and were still influenced by those usages. The first Prime Minister who had not been thus conditioned was Lord Rosebery, but he had never sat in the House of Commons and was, given the precarious circumstances of his brief and unhappy tenure, in no position to dismiss anyone. The second was Balfour (who incidentally is the only Prime Minister to have been President of the British Academy). He was reputed to be easy-going, but he unhesitatingly dismissed a number of his colleagues as the result of a complicated imbroglio in 1903. In fact he overdid it, and the blow to confidence which he thus gave probably contributed in some degree to the landslide of 1906. There was no comparable purge till Mr. Macmillan's in the summer of 1962, and many people both at the time and in retrospect queried the wisdom of that. By the early years of the twentieth century the Prime Minister's power to require the resignation of a minister, whatever the reason, was no longer a matter of doubt. The wisdom of exercising it—or at least of exercising it at all often—was and still is another matter.

The period of governmental instability between the first two Reform Acts, more reminiscent of the French Third and Fourth Republics than the British system of today, began to change in the 1870s. Whether or not it was a matter of cause and effect, the Reform Act of 1867 was followed by a series of general elections which gave far clearer and more decisive results in the House than anything since 1841 and this trend continued after further extensions of the franchise. It was symbolic of the new pattern of politics that in 1868 Disraeli resigned on the morrow of the general election without waiting to test the opinion of the House, so clear had been the verdict of the polls. Some people grumbled and said his conduct was unconstitutional, but Gladstone reluctantly followed the same course in 1874, and Disraeli repeated his action in 1880. Since then it has only been in highly exceptional circumstances (e.g. 1924 or February 1974 when the election result was ambiguous) that a Prime Minister has failed to accept at once what appears to be the decision of the electorate. Even in 1964, despite one or two suggestions to the contrary, Sir Alec Douglas-Home resigned as soon as the results were in, though Labour's victory was by the narrowest margin ever known. But a Prime Minister acts within his rights if he chooses to meet Parliament. Mr. Heath would not have broken any convention of the constitution if, after the election of 28 February 1974, he had decided to do this.

The reason for this instant acceptance of parliamentary arithmetic has of course been the inflexibility of party boundaries and the predictability of the division lobbies. It is a feature of the same development that governments have seldom over the last hundred years fallen to an adverse vote in the House. Gladstone in 1886 and Rosebery in 1895 are exceptions. Ramsay MacDonald was defeated in 1924, and followed the same course with the same result as Gladstone thirty-eight years earlier, viz. dissolution and loss of the election. The last occasion on which the House can be said to have forced the Prime Minister to resign was the fall of Neville Chamberlain in 1940, but he was not actually defeated. It was a massive slump in his normally overwhelming parliamentary majority which decided him to go, and war made it impossible for him to riposte with a dissolution.

From the 1870s onwards party government in the modern sense has prevailed. It was during this period that the mass party organizations in the country established themselves—a recognition that power had shifted to the electorate. Gladstone appreciated the change when he wrote to Rosebery in the 1880s: 'What is outside Parliament seems to me to be fast mounting, nay to have already mounted to an importance much exceeding what is inside.' The Birmingham 'Caucus', the National Union of Conservative Associations—these were the typical institutions of the new era. Prime Ministers had become heads of one or other of two great political parties with electoral committees or associations in almost every constituency. Of course Peel and Melbourne, Russell and Derby had also been leaders of parties but these are better described as parliamentary connections than parties in our modern sense. The difference after 1867 was that Gladstone and

Disraeli led parties which not only operated in Parliament but had spread their roots throughout the country.

By a natural process of development the leaders personally came to symbolize the causes for which they stood. It is often alleged that this personification of politics is a new phenomenon, produced in part by exposure to the mass media. It is no doubt true that every elector nowadays knows what Mr. Heath and Mr. Wilson look like. They would not be as lucky as Peel, who escaped assassination because the lunatic who intended to kill him shot his private secretary instead. But by the time of Gladstone and Disraeli most electors must from cartoons and other representations have had a fair idea of the appearance of the great rivals, and there can be no question that their personalities dominated the whole political scene, not merely, as in the case of Pitt and Fox, the House of Commons. In reference to the passions provoked by the Eastern crisis in 1878 Henry Loch, Governor of the Isle of Man, writing for the benefit of a friend in India said:

... when the questions are discussed, which they are morning, noon and night by all classes and by both sexes there is an intensity of excitement that frequently breaks out in the most violent language—and it is all *purely personal*, the divergence of opinion being not so much upon the merits of the questions which seem seldom understood, but upon the feelings that are entertained either towards Lord Beaconsfield or Mr Gladstone.[1]

There is nothing new during the last hundred years in this polarization of personalities. It depends upon the personalities. There have been many times since the days of Disraeli and Gladstone when it did not apply—for example after Disraeli's death when Northcote and Salisbury opposed Gladstone. Again between 1902 and 1911, when on the one side Balfour, and on the other Campbell-Bannerman and Asquith, led their respective parties, one

[1] Blake, *Disraeli*, p. 761.

may well doubt whether personality was particularly relevant. Forty-five years later with Churchill and Attlee it was; also during the 1960s when first Mr. Macmillan confronted Hugh Gaitskell and later when Sir Alec Douglas-Home and then Mr. Heath confronted Mr. Wilson. But there is no clear trend. We can go back to a time before the great duel between Disraeli and Gladstone and find Lord Shaftesbury writing after the election of 1857. 'There seems to be no measure, no principle, no cry, to influence men's minds and determine elections; it is simply, "Were you or were you not? Are you, or are you not, for Palmerston?"'

The question of personality leads to the question of power—one of the most keenly debated subjects in the historiography of the office of Prime Minister. Are Prime Ministers more powerful now than ever before? Has 'Prime Ministerial' government replaced Cabinet government? If so when has the change taken place? What are the reasons for it? Is it a good thing? How is it related to Presidential government in the American mode? No one can deny that a great change has taken place since the era described by Bagehot. It is perhaps doubtful whether even in his day one could correctly describe the Cabinet as 'a board of control chosen by the legislature' or the Prime Minister as 'elected by the representatives of the people'. Certainly such descriptions had become inadequate by the end of the century. In my next lecture I propose to look at the situation as it seems to me today. Meanwhile I would like to summarize the development down to the accession of Lloyd George.

The status and powers of the Prime Minister gradually changed over the years from Walpole's day to the beginning of the First World War. Turning points in history whether political, constitutional, or economic are very hard to fix. But if it has to be done I suggest three. The first was the crisis of 1782–4. For a number of reasons the position of the Crown in relation to the Cabinet and the Prime Minister changed. Perhaps one could say that the change was from a monarch who was the real head of the executive, an active political force concerned with the day-to-day issues of government to a monarch with a veto—the right to dismiss the Prime Minister and so the right to prevent the implementation of policies he disliked. It was a power which always had to be exercised within limits, and it rested on the potential dichotomy between public and parliamentary opinion—the possibility of an appeal as in 1784 from the latter to the former. This dichotomy is taken for granted as extinct since the extension of the franchise—but, who knows, it may appear again if the current proposal for a referendum sets a precedent for the future.

The second change—and the greatest—was from the King's government to party government. It was this which was symbolized and made apparent by the events of 1834–5. The third change less obvious at the time and less radical, though in the end not less significant, was from government by parties based on parliament to government by parties based on nation-wide organizations. One can date its beginning from the Reform Acts of 1867 and 1884. We have not yet, I suspect, seen its full flowering. The leadership is still firmly in the hands of the Parliamentary parties. The ultimate logic of election by party conference and in the end the creation of a system of primary elections seems a long way off, but who can be sure that it will not come one day?

Be that as it may, the office of Prime Minister had changed by 1916, compared with, say, 1866. That half century had made the Prime Minister in one sense more secure. If he could win an election he could for the next six years rely on a Parliamentary majority and carry the measures to which he was committed, or became committed, without much danger of defeat. Of course he could not take Parliament for granted. That is impossible even today. But he was not likely to be ejected by the sort of Parliamentary revolt which turned out Peel in 1846, Russell in 1852, Aberdeen in 1855, Palmerston in 1858, Derby in 1859, and Russell again in 1866. On the other hand, he was becoming more dependent on the party machine, not so much when in power as in his other shape, leader of the opposition. And little had been done to adapt the office to the necessities of a world in which government was playing an ever-widening part. The machinery creaked. There were no minutes and no set agenda. Conduct of affairs was unbusinesslike. It was often difficult to be sure what the Cabinet had really decided. War is a great catalyst of change which is one of the reasons why all sound Conservatives should avoid it if they can. Two world wars did indeed bring many changes. How deep and how wide their effect will be part of my theme in my next lecture when I try to look at the office of Prime Minister as it has become in the 1970s.

D

III. THE PRESENT

It is not disputed that Bagehot's brilliant picture of the Trollopian Prime Minister's position had already become obsolete—or at least obsolescent—before Bagehot died. He was drawing a portrait which, however shrewd a likeness of the constitutional system as it operated between the Reform Acts of 1832 and 1867, was no longer so true of the period which followed. This is in no way to underestimate the relevance of many of Bagehot's comments to much that occurred after 1867, indeed to much that is occurring even now.

What is obvious, however, is that the relations between Prime Minister, the Cabinet, Parliament, the electorate, the parties, the civil service, the Crown were not the same in the post-1867 era as they had been before. The Premierships of Disraeli, Gladstone, Salisbury, Asquith were conducted under different usages from those of Peel, Russell, Derby, Palmerston. The question which now arises is how far the Premiership has changed yet again, since the end of the half century from 1867 to 1917 when Lloyd George began to establish his own way of running the office.

The most interesting and controversial discussions of this matter are in the late Mr. R. H. S. Crossman's introduction to the new edition of Bagehot's *The English Constitution* published in 1963 just before Mr. Crossman himself became a member of the Labour Cabinet, and in Mr. John McIntosh's *The British Cabinet* (1962). If I refer mainly to Mr. Crossman it is because his is the more arresting and provocative of the two treatments. His theme is that the power of the Prime Minister has enormously increased during and since the Second World War. Bagehot had described the Cabinet as 'the hyphen which joins, the buckle which fastens, the legislative part of the state to the executive'. According to Mr. Crossman that role is now fulfilled by a single man. 'The post war epoch has seen the final transformation of Cabinet Government into Prime Ministerial Government.'

Mr. Crossman discerns three causes for the change. There has been the growth of the power of party which has reduced that of the individual M.P., diminished his chances of defying party orthodoxy, and removed the real debate on political issues 'from the floor of the Commons to the secrecy of the Committee rooms upstairs'. This enhances the power of the Prime Minister in his capacity as the party leader. 'Politics is inevitably personified and simplified in the public mind into a battle between two super-leaders—appointed for life or until they are removed by an intra party *coup d'état.*' Secondly, there was the ending of Cabinet informality by the creation of a secretariat to keep the minutes and circulate papers. This occurred soon after Lloyd George became Prime Minister, and, so Mr. Crossman argues, inevitably enhanced the Prime Minister's powers by giving him what was tantamount to a department of his own.

Lloyd George was also involved in the third of Mr. Crossman's suggested causes of change—the unification of the civil service, with the Permanent Under Secretary of the Treasury at its head. This occurred in September 1919 when Sir Warren Fisher persuaded the Prime Minister that the talents of civil servants would be better recognized and used if people could move from department to department, instead of staying for their whole career in the same one—the prevailing practice hitherto. A further regulation 'laid down that the consent of the Premier (which in practice meant the head of the civil service) would be required in all departments to the appointment of permanent heads and their deputies'. The upshot, so Mr. Crossman argues, was the creation of a 'group of super-bureaucrats each confident that he can take charge at a few weeks' notice of a Ministry of which he has had no previous experience'. This has replaced the old system of a cluster of departments with their own traditions, styles, and methods of recruitment.

Here Mr. Crossman perhaps proves too much. The power of the Prime Minister over his Cabinet colleagues may well have been increased by the unification of the Civil Service, for ministers no longer appoint to the permanent headships of their departments, but Mr. Crossman agrees that it is not really the Prime Minister who takes over that role. In practice it is the head of the Civil Service. So, if the Prime Minister has gained power as regards ministers, can it not be argued also that he has in some measure lost it to the 'super-bureaucrats'? This raises a wider question. Is it clear that Peel who was his own Secretary to the Cabinet and the Treasury and who supervised every department of state, had a less powerful position than Sir Alec Douglas-Home who was operating when the changes described by Mr. Crossman should have had ample time to become fully effective? Prime Ministerial power is not a simple or straightforward concept. There is obviously one sense in which any modern prime minister has more power than Peel, Gladstone, Lloyd George, or Neville Chamberlain, because government itself controls a far wider area of national life than it ever has before. The real question is the balance of power within the governmental system at this or that moment of time. It is doubtful whether the change has been as definite as Mr. Crossman implies. In an illuminating study of the British constitution—*The Body Politic* (1969)—Mr. Ian Gilmour, who like Mr. Crossman came into office subsequently (though on the opposite political side), puts the point clearly.

The writers of the Prime Ministerial school make the same mistake as the Whig historians made about George III and the monarchy: they overrate his power today and underrate the power he had in the past.

The development of the office has not been all one way. The progress towards Caesarism has been uneven and its starting point uncertain.[1]

The point is particularly relevant to another of the features which in Mr. Crossman's view and that of others has increased the power of the Prime Minister, viz. the creation of the Cabinet Secretariat. That this long overdue reform increased the efficiency of government in general is indubitable. The mere fact that formal minutes were taken, after a lapse of some eighty years, in itself made a considerable difference. (It is worth remembering that this was the revival of an old usage not the establishment of a new one. Precisely because the King never presided over the 'efficient Cabinet' he needed a formal minute of its deliberations. The practice seems to have vanished under Melbourne who, in tutoring the young Queen, preferred to inform her by a letter couched in language more suitable for someone so inexperienced than a dry minute.[2] This developed into the regular 'Cabinet letter' from the Prime Minister to the Sovereign—which is our only direct official historical source for the discussions in the Cabinet from the late 1830s till 1917.)

But the establishment of the Cabinet Secretariat did not necessarily augment the power of the Prime Minister. The Secretariat serves the Cabinet as a whole. Contrary to Mr. Crossman's claim, it is not a department of the Prime Minister. If it was, why do Prime Ministers from time to time try to create another department to fulfil that purpose?

[1] p. 206.   [1] E. T. Williams, op. cit.

Not all Prime Ministers do so, but it is interesting that Lloyd George, the very man under whom the Cabinet Secretariat came into being, should have felt the need for a special group of informal advisers in addition to the Cabinet Office proper. This body, known as 'the Garden Suburb' because it worked in temporary huts in the garden of 10 Downing Street, consisted of gifted outsiders sympathetic to Lloyd George; several of them were academics whose profession, in Britain as in the U.S.A., makes them particularly adept at the Byzantine intrigues which so often surround the holders of high office. At the time many people understandably found the 'Garden Suburb' difficult to disentangle from the Cabinet Secretariat; and there was a real danger when Bonar Law came into power in 1922 on a wave of revulsion against Lloyd George that he would throw out the baby with the bathwater and abolish both. At the strong persuasion of Maurice Hankey and Tom Jones, Secretary and Deputy Secretary of the Cabinet, he confined himself to the abolition of the 'Garden Suburb', but it was a near thing.

The next occasion when a similar body came into being was Churchill's so-called 'Statistical Section' under Professor Lindemann (Lord Cherwell) created as a group of personal advisers while Churchill was First Lord of the Admiralty and continuing with him when he became Prime Minister. Its members were mostly distinguished economists such as Sir Roy Harrod and Sir Donald MacDougall, and their task was very far from being confined to statistics. They provided an alternative source of advice and could criticize behind the scenes the advice of the officials. As a result they became extremely unpopular in Whitehall but no one could do anything about them while Churchill was in power. When he lost in 1945 they did not wait to be dismissed but at once resigned with him.

Mr. Wilson, since he came into office early in March

1974, has established what is called a Policy unit to serve something of the same purpose. It too consists largely of academics, headed by Dr. Bernard Donoghue, a Senior Lecturer in Politics at the London School of Economics. It acts as the Prime Minister's eyes and ears. It is not to be confused with the Central Policy Review Staff, the so-called 'Think Tank' created by Mr. Heath, which is concerned with longer-term planning. This, like the Cabinet Secretariat, serves the Cabinet as a whole and is in fact a part of the Cabinet Office.

I do not wish to discuss the success of these experiments, or the somewhat allied subject of the influence of Prime Ministers' private secretaries, and/or *eminences grises*— the role of Monty Corry (Lord Rowton) in Disraeli's affairs, Sir Algernon West in Gladstone's, or the very strange part played by J. S. Sanders in Balfour's life. These are intriguing by-ways of history, but there is no time to pursue them here.

The point is that in spite of the undeniably important changes which have occurred since the First World War it is not clear that the creation of the Cabinet Secretariat and the unification of the Civil Service have had quite the enhancing effect on Prime Ministerial power with which they are sometimes credited. Prime Ministers still seem to feel the need for some other source of advice and knowledge than that provided by the orthodox Whitehall channels. It is certainly arguable that the power of the permanent Civil Service has become greater than it was, but it does not follow that this has increased that of the Prime Minister.

*　　*　　*

Lord Morley in his *Walpole* (1889) said:

The flexibility of the Cabinet system allows the Prime Minister to take upon himself a power not inferior to that of a dictator, provided always that the House of Commons will stand by him.

Morley was writing about the first Prime Minister, but he certainly had in mind the office as he knew it. He had been a member of Gladstone's Cabinet in 1886. He perceived the great power which lay in the hands of someone determined to use it, and also the limitations; the House of Commons did not stand by Gladstone in 1886 and he was defeated on the second reading of the Irish Home Rule Bill.

The truth is that the powers of the Prime Minister have varied with the personality of the Prime Minister or with the particular political circumstances of his tenure. No one has come nearer to Presidential government on the American model than Lloyd George. Yet none of the factors which Mr. Crossman sees as causing this development in the second half of the twentieth century applied then. The Cabinet Secretariat and the unification of the Civil Service were indeed the results of decisions by Lloyd George but they cannot have had much effect before 1922. As for the position of the Prime Minister as leader of his party, Lloyd George was especially ill-placed. He led no party, only a Liberal splinter group. In the end this weakness was fatal, but it did not handicap him at the height of his prestige when, after virtually abolishing in wartime the old Cabinet system, he told Austen Chamberlain, perhaps half in jest, that he thought of doing without the Cabinet altogether in peacetime, when he conducted foreign policy through a private office of his own, by-passing the indignant Lord Curzon, and when he effortlessly dominated the House of Commons, carrying his way on almost every issue.

Lloyd George was not the first Prime Minister to treat his Cabinet in a cavalier way. Campbell-Bannerman never revealed to the full Cabinet the staff conversations with the French initiated in December 1905 by Sir Edward Grey, although he was well aware of their far-reaching implications. His latest biographer, Mr. John Wilson, considers that this was a deliberate decision taken in order to avoid a row with the radical wing of the ministry. In 1877, during the Russo-Turkish war, an even more striking instance of Prime Ministerial secrecy occurred. Disraeli had tried to persuade the Cabinet to issue an ultimatum to Russia, threatening war in the event of a second Russian campaign against Turkey in the spring of the following year. The Cabinet, as so often at that time, would neither agree nor disagree. Disraeli, accordingly sent a secret emissary to St. Petersburg to inform the Tsar that the Cabinet was entirely united in its determination to go to war, if there was a second campaign. The other ministers, including the Foreign Secretary, were kept in ignorance of this *démarche* by their chief, and some of them would undoubtedly have raised the strongest objections had they known.

Modern Prime Ministers have been much more 'correct'. Oddly enough the two instances of Prime Ministerial indifference to Cabinet responsibility quoted by Mr. Crossman do not really support his case. He makes much of Attlee's alleged by-passing of the Cabinet over the construction of the atomic bomb, but the facts do not substantiate the charge. The decision, it is true, was taken by the Defence Sub-committee of the Cabinet, but the minutes were circulated to all members of the Cabinet. Moreover, it was communicated to Parliament in answer to a question on 12 May 1948. His other example is Anthony Eden and the Suez crisis. The facts here are more obscure, but it seems on balance that, although some ministers may have felt that they had been 'bounced', the correct constitutional procedure was formally followed. No doubt much more was known by some than others, and the detailed planning was done by a group in close sympathy with Anthony Eden's aims. This, however, is common form. Neville Chamberlain constituted with himself, Lord Halifax, Sir

John Simon, and Sir Samuel Hoare just such a group at the time of Munich in 1938. In every Cabinet some ministers are more equal than others.

Another point made by the prime-ministerial school is the increased use made of Cabinet committees. In fact their existence is quite old. There was a Crimean Committee in 1855, and a Cabinet Committee to draft the abortive Reform Act of 1859. In the First World War Lloyd George made much use of committees (with a small war cabinet of five or six he had to). It largely lapsed in the inter-war years, to be revived again in the Second World War; and it has been continued since. But it is by no means clear that this procedure makes the Prime Minister a more dominant force. It could be equally well argued that it strengthens— by making more efficient—the Cabinet itself. At all events the balance is not obvious.

I have considered the changes of the present day in the relations of the Prime Minister with his party, his cabinet, Parliament, and the Civil Service. There is a fourth element in the constitution to be considered—the Crown. I have already discussed certain aspects of the decline in the power of the Crown, from the reign of George II through his grandson and his two great grandsons to the end of the reign of Queen Victoria. By then it really narrowed down to two things: the selection of the Prime Minister in certain circumstances and the right to refuse a dissolution (the right to force one had disappeared if it ever existed). Let us take each in turn.

Formally of course the Crown always appoints the Prime Minister. Practically—in nine cases out of ten—the monarch's choice is limited to the leader of the majority party in the House of Commons. But there have been circumstances in which a genuine element of choice enters in. It is, moreover, a well-established constitutional doctrine that the choice of a Prime Minister is one of the few acts in which the Crown is not bound by 'advice' in the constitutional sense of the word. If a Prime Minister resigns through defeat, there is by definition no Prime Minister to give advice. Anyway it would be absurd if he were in a position to give binding advice on the choice of Prime Minister from the opposing party. But equally if he dies, or resigns for some other reason than defeat, there is no one who can give binding advice. Of course the monarch can consult an out-going Prime Minister and could accept his advice. That might be a perfectly sensible thing to do, but the advice would be accepted on the Crown's responsibility. It could not be made the responsibility—in the constitutional sense—of the departing Prime Minister. What is clear is that the Prime Minister cannot, as of right, fix the succession. There is no such thing in that sense as a 'Deputy Prime Minister', although Prime Ministers have from time to time tried to create an office with these implications.

At the end of Queen Victoria's reign the practical element of choice was made possible by three features of public life, two of which have disappeared but the third of which could still be relevant. First the House of Commons and the House of Lords were near enough to being equipollent for a peer to be Prime Minister, so that the party which had won an election could have two potential occupants of 10 Downing Street, its leader in the Commons or its leader in the Lords. This is not true now. Nor even then would it in itself have given any freedom of choice, for nineteenth-century political parties might have invented some sort of machinery by which they elected a single leader. In practice they did not and the fact is a reminder of the strictly parliamentary origin of our political parties. In practice each House elected its own leader, and there was no process of joint election. This is the second feature which has now disappeared, for a system of election whether in power or opposition now exists in all the political parties.

The usage in Queen Victoria's reign was that, if a party in opposition had in either House an ex-Prime Minister still active in politics and leading his party in that House, he had the prior claim to office when the party returned to power. There could have been no serious question of the Queen sending for any one except Peel in 1841, Disraeli in 1874, Salisbury in 1886, Gladstone in 1892 (though in the last case she fought as hard as she could against 'that dangerous old fanatic', as she privately termed him). On the other hand, in 1885 she had a real choice. Disraeli had died four years earlier. There was no living Tory ex-Prime Minister. She could choose between Salisbury, leader of the Lords and Northcote, leader of the Commons. She chose Salisbury, but no one could have said that she would have been acting unconstitutionally if she had chosen Northcote.

When a Prime Minister resigned through ill health or died in office—Gladstone in 1894, Palmerston in 1865— a slightly different but not dissimilar situation arose. By definition there was no available ex-Prime Minister. There was a leader of the House to which the late Prime Minister had not belonged, and there might be a semi-established second-in-command in the House to which he had belonged. This was the situation in 1894 when the choice lay between Rosebery and Harcourt. Obviously the reality of every such choice turned on the personalities involved, the readiness of A to serve under B, or C to serve under either of them. When Lord Derby bowed himself out in March 1868 the Queen might theoretically have chosen a prominent peer, but clearly Disraeli was the only plausible choice because he obviously carried more influence and prestige (however much some people of his party disliked him) than anyone else. In the case of Rosebery and Harcourt the balance was much more even.

The question of choosing between the leaders of the two Houses gradually faded out as a real issue in the 1920s. The case of Lord Halifax in 1940 was very abnormal. But there remained another option which could arise when a Prime Minister with a majority in the House resigned through ill health. The Conservative party had no machinery for electing its leader in such an eventuality. It had been obliged to improvise one for electing a leader of the Parliamentary party when in opposition. This was done in 1911 when Balfour retired and Bonar Law was elected. But from then until 1965 no case occurred of a Conservative leader retiring while in the position of 'shadow' Prime Minister. The changes that took place occurred when the party was in office, and the Crown made the appointment. This could involve a real element of discretion, not so much in assessing the merits of candidates as in ascertaining, despite the lack of any elective system, whom the party wanted. Once again it was a matter of personalities. There was no real choice in 1938 when Chamberlain succeeded Baldwin, or in 1955 when Eden succeeded Churchill. There was a real choice, on the other hand, on two occasions (even if we set aside the Curzon/ Baldwin affair of 1923); the appointment of Mr. Macmillan in 1957 and of Sir Alec Douglas-Home in 1963.

These decisions have been the subject of much controversy but it is not likely that this particular form of monarchical choice will come up again. The Labour party, which has never so far been confronted with the problem of a successor to its leadership while in office, made it clear in 1957, adopting a Conservative precedent—Bonar Law in 1922—that the Parliamentary party would expect no one to accept office before he had been duly elected as leader. Bonar Law's precedent had not been followed by the Conservatives. Neither Baldwin in 1923 nor Chamberlain in 1938 felt obliged to seek this sort of prior confirmation, but since 1965 the party has had its own electoral procedure. This seems to rule out royal choice altogether. No political party will expect to have its selection pre-empted by the Crown, although the Conservative system might be dangerously slow and cumbrous if a Conservative Prime Minister died or resigned in the middle of a serious political crisis.[1]

Yet can one even now, despite these changes, argue that the role of the monarch is purely mechanical, and that no element of discretion survives at all? I am not quite convinced that this is so even today. No doubt the cases of 1957 and 1963 were in a sense anachronistic. It was odd that the Conservative party had not devised an electoral procedure much earlier, and its failure to do so was—one may guess—an embarrassment to the Crown which was obliged in effect to find out what the party wanted, by indirect means where direct would have been more desirable. For there has, on the evidence available, been a change since 1900 in the attitude of the Crown. When Queen Victoria chose Rosebery she did so because she thought he would be the better Prime Minister, not because she thought he would be the most acceptable leader of the Liberal party. When King George V chose Baldwin, when Queen Elizabeth II chose Mr. Macmillan and Sir Alec Douglas-Home, they did so because those were the men who, they were advised, would command most support in the Conservative party. It is a matter of controversy how correct that advice was in each case. My own guess is that it was as sound as such advice ever can be, but there is clearly a powerful argument for obliging the party to make up its own mind through its own chosen procedure.

[1] The latest proposed emendations (December 1974) make the process potentially even slower, and there could be a delay of nearly three weeks. It is clearly desirable that the implications should be considered by the Conservative leadership, and there is reason to believe that they soon will be.

Yet the disappearance of this sort of royal choice does not mean that all choice has vanished or that no Prime Minister can ever be appointed except by the majority vote of the majority party. There have been three clear cases this century where Prime Ministers have been appointed, although they were not, and in two of the cases had no prospect of being, elected leaders of their respective parties; Lloyd George in 1916, Ramsay Mac-Donald in 1931, Winston Churchill in 1940. I do not think one can wholly exclude the possibility of a crisis in which royal discretion might have to be invoked in order that government can be carried on at all—a situation in which the mechanical application of automatic rules simply could not work.

The other field in which the Crown must surely, despite certain cries from the left of the Parliamentary Labour party in May 1974, have some discretion is the granting of a dissolution of Parliament. This is a matter of such complication and so little understood that it is worth a brief discussion. In one sense the practice of the last sixty years has enhanced the power of the Prime Minister. Until the First World War no one doubted that the decision to advise the Crown to dissolve Parliament was a collective decision of the Cabinet, or at any rate of those members of it who sit in the House of Commons. (When Disraeli took the opinion of his Cabinet in 1880 on the question of dissolution, only the Commoners gave voice, but whether this was a normal practice I do not know. In any case it was a Cabinet decision.) For reasons which are not wholly clear the practice since 1918 has been for the decision to rest with the Prime Minister alone, taking such advice (or none) as he sees fit. The Cabinet was not consulted over the timing of the Coupon Election nor, as far as is publicly known, has it been consulted since.

Quite why and when the change occurred is a bit of

a puzzle. Asquith in his *Fifty Years of Parliament*[1] was emphatic that 'such a question as the dissolution of Parliament is always submitted to the Cabinet for ultimate decision'. Yet Balfour writing to Bonar Law apropos of the question of dissolving in 1918 said:

I think that, whatever happens, the responsibility of a dissolution must rest with the Prime Minister. It always does so rest in fact; and on some previous occasions the Prime Minister of the day has not even gone through the form of consulting his colleagues.[2]

This conflict almost suggests that Liberal and Conservative usage had been different, but the evidence in fact seems to support Asquith. The decision to hold the 'Khaki' Election of 1900 was certainly taken by the Conservative Cabinet and Balfour himself must have been present.

Bonar Law, however, accepted Balfour's view for he put the responsibility on to Lloyd George. He may also have been influenced by his own experience in 1916. He was then asked to form a government—which he declined to do in the end. The King made it clear when inviting him to take office that he would not promise in advance a dissolution to a hypothetical or potential Prime Minister. He would only consider it from a Prime Minister actually in office. But the language used by the King could easily have suggested that it was only the Prime Minister who was concerned, and Bonar Law, still comparatively inexperienced in these matters, may have drawn the wrong conclusion. Another possibility is that so very 'political' a matter as the timing of a dissolution came to be regarded as an awkward matter to discuss in Cabinet in front of officials, whereas before the war there were no officials present.

Whatever the reason it seems clear that the responsibility now lies with the Prime Minister alone. No doubt

---

[1] ii, p. 195.
[2] Quoted from Balfour Papers, Blake, *Unknown Prime Minister* (1955), p. 385.

E

the point is usually academic. No Prime Minister would take such a decision without informally consulting his principal colleagues and getting their support. But there could be freak cases. In 1969 it was widely rumoured that Mr. Wilson was at odds with his leading colleagues and was contemplating a dissolution despite their strongly felt opinion to the contrary. Nothing came of it and the rumour may have been baseless, but, if such a division were to be obvious and public, what is the duty of the Crown? Suppose we had a Prime Minister who was ill or had a nervous breakdown. It has happened. Both Chatham and his son suffered from something very like that on occasions in their lives. And, irrespectively of health, must the Crown accept unconditionally advice to dissolve in the knowledge that the great majority of ministers are strongly against it? In somewhat analogous circumstances the Governor-General of South Africa refused a dissolution to Herzog in 1939 and appointed General Smuts instead.

This brings us to the wider question of the Crown's position with regard to a dissolution. When on 25 March 1974 the *Tribune* group raised the matter with Mr. Edward Short, they wrote: 'In our opinion the Prime Minister of the day has an absolute right to decide the date of the election, following discussion with his Cabinet colleagues.'[1] The observation about discussion with colleagues presumably refers to the alleged events of 1969. Mr. Short did not take it up in his reply on 9 May, but he was quite categorical in regarding the general doctrine of the *Tribune* group as unacceptable.

Constitutional lawyers of the highest authority are of the clear opinion that the Sovereign is not in all circumstances bound to grant a Prime Minister's request for a dissolution. But the exercise of the royal prerogative in this matter is not determined only by past constitutional usages and precedents: the

[1] *The Times*, 11 May 1974.

relevance of those usages and precedents has to be considered in relation to the actual circumstances.[1]

It followed that one could not define in advance the circumstances in which the Sovereign's discretion might be exercised. There the matter rests. The attempt to get it debated in the House did not succeed.

This is far from being a purely academic matter. It arose from the possibility that Mr. Wilson might be defeated on the Address in reply to the Queen's Speech on 18 March, and ask for an immediate dissolution. He behaved as if he was confident that it would be granted, and the Conservatives at the last moment seem to have become convinced that it would. There is at present no means of knowing for certain what was the truth. No doubt it will emerge in due course. What, however, is quite clear is that in those circumstances the Queen was not obliged to grant a dissolution even if she was not obliged not to. The determining factor may well have been the failure of the overture already made by Mr. Heath to the Liberals, which must have made it seem unlikely that a stable majority could be formed out of any other ingredients; in that case having refused a dissolution to Mr. Wilson she might have had to grant it to his successor. To take a more extreme case, suppose Mr. Heath had himself decided to meet Parliament, as he was entitled to do, and suppose that opinion polls or some other cause led him to believe that a quick election would reverse the previous one, could he have claimed a dissolution if he had been beaten on the Queen's Speech? Surely this would have been a case where the Crown would have had every justification in refusing.

Although for a very long time past there has been no instance of the Crown refusing a dissolution to a British Prime Minister, Governors-General of Dominions and

[1] *The Times*, 11 May 1974.

Governors or Lieutenant-Governors of States within a Federal Dominion have refused requests from their Prime Ministers. Their position is perhaps not quite the same as that of the Crown since they hold office for a limited tenure and do not have to live with the problem for an indefinite period, but otherwise it is very similar. And there has been at least one clear case in Britain where the Crown would have refused a dissolution to a minority Prime Minister if the leaders of the other parties had been willing to join forces. This was when Ramsay MacDonald, after his tenth defeat in Parliament, asked for a dissolution in October 1924—the third general election within two years. The King sounded out Baldwin and Asquith, but finding them uninterested in a coalition had no option but to grant the dissolution.

The position of a minority government is perhaps different in this respect from that of one with a majority. But I am not clear that the Crown is bound to accept advice for a dissolution even from the latter in all circumstances automatically. What if Mr. Wilson were to ask for another election before Christmas?[1] Nor is it certain that the Crown's power to choose a Prime Minister is entirely defunct. What happens if the Cabinet breaks up because of a grave national crisis? There have already been two elections and the Prime Minister asks for a third within eighteen months. A large majority of his colleagues are in favour of a coalition. A small minority follow him in the view that they will not have it at any price and prefer a dissolution. Is the Queen bound to accept the Prime Minister's advice? Or could she seek for an alternative Prime Minister? I should say at once that these contingencies seem to me very improbable, but the electoral deadlock of 28 February 1974 seemed highly improbable too. These freaks and chances cannot be ruled out as

[1] This lecture was delivered on 24 October 1974.

inconceivable though one hopes that the Crown will not in practice be confronted with such a difficult dilemma. But the Crown does still remain, despite its greatly diminished constitutional status since even Queen Victoria's, let alone George III's reign, a sort of reserve power which in certain circumstances might affect the way in which the Prime Minister operates.

We live in an era when many of our time-honoured constitutional usages are being scrutinized and questioned. It is not the first occasion nor is it necessarily a sign that they are obsolete or that they are on their way out. Such scepticism is more commonly a symptom of a general malaise which may be only temporary—an uneasiness about the social, political, or economic problems which face the nation and which seem insoluble within its existing constitutional framework. They may of course be equally insoluble in any other framework. They may in the course of time just go away. But for the moment they seem beyond the scope of the established order which is accordingly blamed for inadequacy, inefficiency, and inability to deal with the great questions of the day. Twice before in this century we have been through similar periods of stress and anxiety accompanied by similar misgivings about the governmental system.

The first was in the years just before the First World War. Britain's apparently declining status as a great power, the emergence of labour as a social force, the bitterness engendered by the Irish problem, all contributed to a feeling that the parliamentary system was no longer able to cope. There was syndicalism on the left, an incipient Caesarism on the right, and that curious amalgam of anti-semitism and Catholic authoritarianism represented by Belloc and the Chestertons which was neither right nor left but was strongly anti-parliamentarian. The charge against the system was not just incompetence, it was also corruption. And, as often happens, something occurred which seemed to justify the accusation. The Marconi Scandal was what the Poulson affair has been in our own time. Although a fascinating story not wholly unravelled even now, it was not really very significant, an accident of personalities which came to be regarded as a symptom and a symbol.

Twenty years later Britain went through another crisis of doubt about the efficacy of the system. Once again the danger seemed both external and internal; the threat of a resurgent Germany, the seemingly insoluble problem of poverty, unemployment, and depression. Once again institutions were blamed. No less a man than Winston Churchill advocated a 'parliament of industry'. Harold Laski considered that socialism could only be achieved by some general enabling Act after which Parliament would be largely by-passed. He doubted whether the civil service, the military, the police could be relied on to carry out a Labour party's policy even if the party had a majority in the Commons. From other quarters came frankly authoritarian criticisms. There was Sir Oswald Mosley and his British Union of Fascists. There was the Communist party which proselytized—anyway among the intelligentsia— more effectively than ever before or since.

No historical situation repeats itself, but there are obvious similarities between both these situations and that of today. For over ten years past the Parliamentary system within which successive governments have operated has not provided the framework for a solution to the endemic economic malady of Britain. An adverse balance of payments, lagging productivity, and chronic inflation have not yet yielded to any of the measures so far attempted. It is not surprising that the parliamentary and party system has come increasingly under fire, especially when one adds to these internal problems the stresses intangible but not less real produced by the passing of empire and the decline of power. It is not to be expected that, if there are misgivings about the Parliamentary system, the office of Prime Minister which is one of its most characteristic features will wholly escape criticism.

Yet having said that, I venture also to say that the Premiership is not in the front of the line being fired at. It is perfectly possible—though by no means certain— that substantial changes will be made during the next ten years in our traditional constitutional arrangements. There could be major experiments in devolution, even some form of quasi-federalism. There could be some type of P.R. But, even if the biggest of those potential changes were to be made in the shape of a drastic reform of the electoral system such as is understandably demanded by the minority parties, I doubt whether it would greatly affect the working of the office of Prime Minister.

No doubt it would produce coalition governments. 'England does not love coalitions', Disraeli said in 1852. What he meant was that he did not love the coalition which was about to turn out the Tory Cabinet of which he was a member. Whether or not England loves coalitions, England has frequently had to put up with them. In the last eighty years we have been governed more often by a coalition than by one of the parties on their own. The administrations of Salisbury and Balfour from 1895 to 1905 were coalitions.[1] There were the war and post-war coalitions of 1915 to 1922; and we were governed by a coalition from 1931 to 1945. I am not putting in a plea for coalitions or pronouncing on whether or not those particular examples were good or bad. I am merely saying that the British Cabinet of which the Prime Minister is the keystone can accommodate such a situation. Some prophets of doom are claiming that we are on the verge of a

[1] Of Conservatives and Liberal Unionists.

complete collapse of our traditional parliamentary system. 'This may be like the last parliament of a Weimar Republic', an elder statesman said to me recently. But unless we are really in such a parlous state—and I for one do not believe that we are—the office of Prime Minister will survive, modified perhaps in minor ways but broadly in the shape and form as it is today. I would be surprised if in 1984 it will be working very differently from 1974; just as it is not now working very differently from 1964 or 1954.

It would be nice if these lectures had produced some startling new truths about the premiership. I would not claim any such achievement. What seems most clearly to emerge is the extraordinary variety of people who have held the office and of the ways in which they have conducted affairs. Obviously there have been some important changes which have altered the constitutional framework within which the Prime Minister operated and I have tried to sketch these over the years. The positions of the various organs of government in relation to one another are not the same as they were a hundred years ago, and they were not the same in 1874 as they had been fifty, let alone a hundred years before that. The enormous extension of the powers of government, in Britain as in all countries, in itself changes the role of the Prime Minister, just as it has changed that of the President of France or the President of the United States.

Yet the position of the Prime Minister in terms of an internal balance of power has altered only slowly and over long periods of time. The differences, if we take any half century, or even more, are largely between personalities—the way in which this or that occupant of 10 Downing Street in the light of his own circumstances feels that he should or can or wants to behave. Lord Liverpool was described some forty years after his death as the last Prime

Minister to have governed Britain. A few months later Goderich was in office, 'a transient and embarrassed phantom' who lasted a few months and resigned before he met Parliament. Or consider the Duke of Portland at the head of the Fox–North Coalition in 1783, who was sometimes not even notified of the meetings of the Cabinet over which he was supposed to preside, and compare him with his successor, Pitt who, as I said earlier, is known to have written the minutes of a Cabinet meeting in advance of its actual occurrence. Or contrast Peel, who supervised every department of State, with Lord Aberdeen only seven years later, the feeble head of the Crimean Coalition.

I would end on the plea that the study of an office such as this depends very largely on the study of individuals. This must be the excuse for some of the slightly frivolous personal statistics which I gave in my first lecture. Political science can certainly teach us to make some generalizations. Constitutional law can tell us what are the wide limits within which the incumbent can operate. But at the end of it all there remains the study of particular statesmen and particular circumstances. Emerson said 'there is properly no history only biography'. In some branches of historical study the truth of this dictum would be very questionable; but the history of the Premiership is in a very real sense the history of those who have held the office. That must be the excuse for someone who is a biographer rather than a political scientist delivering these lectures.

IV. PRIME MINISTERS OF GREAT BRITAIN

PRIME MINISTERS have normally held the office of First Lord of the Treasury. When a different office was held, e.g. Lord Privy Seal or Secretary of State, the fact is indicated below. Until 1841 the First Lord of the Treasury, if a commoner, nearly always doubled his office with the Chancellorship of the Exchequer, and this is shown by an asterisk. The outstanding exception was the elder Pitt who never held either post.

The attribution of party labels must be to some extent arbitrary. The two-party system under William III and Anne was extinguished by the collapse of the Tories after 1715. From Walpole to the Fox–North Coalition a single-party system prevailed, and it seems better to give no label at all. I have chosen the younger Pitt's as the first Tory government, not because he ever called himself a Tory but because his administration came to be regarded in retrospect as the political progenitor of the line of descent through Perceval, Liverpool, and Wellington. Likewise Lord Grenville's administration of 1806–7 was regarded as the ancestor of Grey's Whig government of 1830. Arguably 'Pittite' and 'Foxite' would be more appropriate labels in the early stages of the transition to a two-party system.

The change from Tory to Conservative and Whig to Liberal is rather more straightforward. I have followed the tradition which makes Peel's government of 1834–5 the first Conservative and Russell's of 1846–52 the last Whig administration.

*Sir Robert Walpole	3 Apr. 1721–11 Feb. 1742
The Earl of Wilmington (died 2 July 1743)	16 Feb. 1742–2 July 1743
*The Hon. Henry Pelham (became Chancellor of the Exchequer from 12 Dec. 1743)	25 Aug. 1743–10 Feb. 1746
The Earl of Bath	10–12 Feb. 1746
*The Hon. Henry Pelham (died 6 Mar. 1754)	13 Feb. 1746–6 Mar. 1754
The Duke of Newcastle	6 Mar. 1754–26 Oct. 1756
William Pitt 'the Elder' (Secretary of State, Southern Department)	16 Nov. 1756–6 Apr. 1757
The Duke of Devonshire	6 Apr.–8 June 1757
Earl Waldegrave	8–12 June 1757
The Duke of Devonshire	12–29 June 1757
William Pitt 'the Elder' (Secretary of State, Southern Department)	29 June 1757–5 Oct. 1761
The Duke of Newcastle	5 Oct. 1761–26 May 1762
The Earl of Bute	26 May 1762–8 Apr. 1763
*George Grenville	10 Apr. 1763–10 July 1765
The Marquess of Rockingham	10 July 1765–12 July 1766
William Pitt 'the Elder' created Earl of Chatham 4 Aug. 1766 (Lord Privy Seal)	30 July 1766–12 Mar. 1767[1]
The Duke of Grafton	12 Mar. 1767–28 Jan. 1770
*Lord North	28 Jan. 1770–20 Mar. 1782
The Marquess of Rockingham (died 1 July 1782)	27 Mar.–1 July 1782
The Earl of Shelburne	3 July 1782–24 Feb. 1783
The Duke of Portland —the Fox–North Coalition	2 Apr.–19 Dec. 1783

[1] Chatham's mental and physical health collapsed after 12 March for nearly two years. Although he remained as Lord Privy Seal until 14 October 1768, the real Prime Minister was the Duke of Grafton from March 1767 onwards.

*The Hon. William Pitt 'the Younger', *Tory*	19 Dec. 1783–14 Mar. 1801
*Henry Addington, *Tory*	14 Mar. 1801–10 May 1804
The Hon. William Pitt 'the Younger', *Tory* (died 23 Jan. 1806)	10 May 1804–23 Jan. 1806
Lord Grenville, *Whig* –'All the Talents'	11 Feb. 1806–25 Mar. 1807
The Duke of Portland, *Tory*	31 Mar. 1807–6 Sept. 1809
*Spencer Perceval, *Tory* (assassinated in House of Commons, 11 May 1812)	4 Oct. 1809–11 May 1812
The Earl of Liverpool, *Tory*	8 June 1812–17 Feb. 1827
*George Canning, *Tory* (died 8 Aug. 1827)	10 Apr. 1827–8 Aug. 1827
Viscount Goderich, *Tory*	31 Aug. 1827–8 Jan. 1828
The Duke of Wellington, *Tory*	22 Jan. 1828–15 Nov. 1830
Earl Grey, *Whig*	16 Nov. 1830–9 July 1834
Viscount Melbourne, *Whig*	16 July 1834–17 Nov. 1834
The Duke of Wellington, *Tory*	17 Nov. 1834–10 Dec. 1834
*Sir Robert Peel, Bart., *Conservative*	10 Dec. 1834–8 Apr. 1835
Viscount Melbourne, *Whig*	18 Apr. 1835–30 Aug. 1831
Sir Robert Peel, Bart., *Conservative*	30 Aug. 1841–30 June 1846
Lord John Russell, *Whig*	30 June 1846–23 Feb. 1852
The Earl of Derby, *Conservative*	23 Feb. 1852–19 Dec. 1852
The Earl of Aberdeen, *Coalition*	19 Dec. 1852–1 Feb. 1855
Viscount Palmerston, *Whig-Liberal*	6 Feb. 1855–19 Feb. 1858
The Earl of Derby, *Conservative*	26 Feb. 1858–10 June 1859
Viscount Palmerston, *Whig-Liberal* (died 18 Oct. 1865)	12 June 1859–18 Oct. 1865
Earl Russell, *Whig-Liberal*	29 Oct. 1865–26 June 1866

The Earl of Derby, *Conservative*	6 July 1966–25 Feb. 1868
Benjamin Disraeli, *Conservative*	28 Feb. 1868–3 Dec. 1868
William Ewart Gladstone, *Liberal*	3 Dec. 1868–17 Feb. 1874
Benjamin Disraeli,[1] *Conservative* (created Earl of Beaconsfield 12 Aug. 1876)	20 Feb. 1874–18 Apr. 1880
*William Ewart Gladstone,[2] *Liberal*	23 Apr. 1880–23 June 1885
The Marquess of Salisbury, *Conservative* (Foreign Secretary)	23 June 1885–27 Jan. 1886
William Ewart Gladstone, *Liberal*	1 Feb. 1886–20 July 1886
The Marquess of Salisbury,[3] *Conservative* (Foreign Secretary from 12 Jan. 1887)	25 July 1886–11 Aug. 1892
William Ewart Gladstone, *Liberal*	15 Aug. 1892–3 Mar. 1894
The Earl of Rosebery, *Liberal*	5 Mar. 1894–25 June 1895
The Marquess of Salisbury,[4] *Conservative* (Foreign Secretary until 1 Nov. 1900)	25 June 1895–12 July 1902
Arthur Balfour, *Conservative*	12 July 1902–4 Dec. 1905
Sir Henry Campbell- Bannerman, *Liberal*	5 Dec. 1905–7 Apr. 1908

[1] From August 1876 to February 1878 Disraeli also held the office of Lord Privy Seal.

[2] Gladstone was Chancellor of the Exchequer till December 1882.

[3] Lord Salisbury reassumed the Foreign Office after Lord Iddesleigh's death on 12 January 1887. W. H. Smith and, in 1891, Arthur Balfour held the office of First Lord of the Treasury.

[4] Lord Salisbury relinquished the Foreign Office on 1 November 1900 and sat in the Cabinet as Lord Privy Seal till his resignation on 12 July 1902.

Herbert Henry Asquith,[1] *Liberal*	7 Apr. 1908–26 May 1915
Herbert Henry Asquith, *Coalition*	26 May 1915–7 Dec. 1916
David Lloyd George, *Coalition*	7 Dec. 1916–19 Oct. 1922
Andrew Bonar Law, *Conservative*	23 Oct. 1922–20 May 1923
*Stanley Baldwin,[2] *Conservative*	22 May 1923–22 Jan. 1924
James Ramsay MacDonald,[3] *Labour*	22 Jan. 1924–4 Nov. 1924
Stanley Baldwin, *Conservative*	4 Nov. 1924–5 June 1929
James Ramsay MacDonald, *Labour*	5 June 1929–24 Aug. 1931
James Ramsay MacDonald, *National Government*	25 Aug. 1931–7 June 1935
Stanley Baldwin, *National Government*	7 June 1935–28 May 1937
Neville Chamberlain, *National Government*	28 May 1937–10 May 1940
Winston Churchill,[4] *Coalition*	10 May 1940–23 May 1945
Winston Churchill, *Conservative* 'Caretaker'	23 May 1945–26 July 1945
Clement Attlee, *Labour*	26 July 1945–26 Oct. 1951
Winston Churchill, *Conservative*	26 Oct. 1951–5 Apr. 1955
Sir Anthony Eden, *Conservative*	6 Apr. 1955–9 Jan. 1957
Harold Macmillan, *Conservative*	10 Jan. 1957–13 Oct. 1963

[1] Asquith was Secretary of State for War from 30 March to 5 August 1914.

[2] Baldwin was Chancellor of the Exchequer till 27 August 1923.

[3] MacDonald was Foreign Secretary as well as First Lord of the Treasury throughout his first administration.

[4] Churchill was Minister of Defence throughout the Coalition and Caretaker administrations, and again from 28 October 1951 to 1 March 1952.

Sir Alec Douglas-Home, *Conservative*	18 Oct. 1963–16 Oct. 1964
Harold Wilson, *Labour*	16 Oct. 1964–19 June 1970
Edward Heath, *Conservative*	19 June 1970–3 Mar. 1974
Harold Wilson, *Labour*	3 Mar. 1974–